Let the Children Come

"*Let the Children Come* is long overdue because our children are vulnerable and abuse is happening. Being proactive at prevention as well as responding to disclosures of abuse in Christ-like ways is the responsibility of the church. Jeanette Harder addresses the tough issues head on, provides valuable insight and the opportunity for dialogue on this often avoided topic. This book offers valuable equipping tools for all congregations."
—Jane Woelk, Voices for Non-Violence, Mennonite Central Committee Manitoba

"Jeanette Harder has given concerned individuals, groups, and congregations an important resource about protecting children and becoming advocates for their well-being. This book is substantive enough for college classes on abuse and yet is written in a style that makes it appropriate for a Sunday school class or small group. This will be a valuable tool for helping make our homes, churches, and communities safer places for children."
—Carolyn Holderread Heggen, author of *Sexual Abuse in Christian Homes and Churches*

Let the Children Come

Preparing Faith Communities

to End Child Abuse and Neglect

Jeanette Harder

Herald Press
Scottdale, Pennsylvania
Waterloo, Ontario

Library of Congress Cataloging-in-Publication Data
Harder, Jeanette, 1964-
    Let the children come : preparing faith communities to end child abuse and
neglect / Jeanette Harder.
        p. cm.
    Includes bibliographical references (p.   ).
    ISBN 978-0-8361-9518-7 (pbk. : alk. paper)
    1. Church work with children—Textbooks. 2. Child abuse—Religious
aspects—Christianity—Textbooks. I. Title.
    BV639.C4H34 2010
    261.8'3271—dc22

                                                    2010031733

Unless otherwise indicated, all Scripture quotations are taken from the *Holy
Bible, New Living Translation*, copyright © 1996, 2004. Used by permission
of Tyndale House Publishers, Inc., Wheaton, Illinois 60189.

Contents

Foreword

In 1976, when asked to comment on child abuse prevention efforts, then director of the U.S. Administration on Children, Youth and Families. (ACYF) Edward Zigler labeled such efforts as doomed to failure. "Social change," he wrote, "is produced not by the stroke of a pen but by intensive and persistent efforts to change the human ecology in which the social target is embedded."[1] Despite his dire warnings, child maltreatment has progressed from a relatively obscure medical condition to a discrete and well-recognized social dilemma.

More importantly, child abuse prevention programs have grown exponentially over the past thirty years. Some of this expansion reflects new public policies and expanded formal services such as parent education classes, support groups, home visitation programs and safety education for children. In other cases, prevention efforts have emanated from the actions of individuals, working on their own and in partnership with others to support their neighbors and to protect children. Rather than rely solely on government solutions to preventing child abuse, individuals have found ways to strengthen local institutions and to build a sense of mutual reciprocity, often by drawing on the resources of their faith communities.

Recent research tracking the number of child abuse cases across the country suggests these efforts are having an impact. For example, the *Fourth Federal National Incidence Study on Child Maltreatment (NIS 4)* reported a 19 percent reduction in the overall rate of child maltreatment since 1993.[2] This reflects substantial and significant drops in the rates of sexual abuse, physical abuse, and emotional abuse. These trends mirror a comparable reduction in the number of such cases being reported each year to local child welfare agencies.[3] These trends demonstrate that child abuse is neither inevitable nor intractable.

Despite the fact that some forms of abuse are less prevalent today, the problem remains substantial, particularly for those children at highest risk for chronic mistreatment and those who experience the greatest harm. In 2007 over three million children were reported as potential victims of maltreatment and almost 1,600 children—or over four children a day—were identified as fatal victims of maltreatment.[4]

These statistics highlight the need for an even greater emphasis on prevention and underscore the importance of engaging the public through diverse methods and diverse institutions. As Jeanette Harder has outlined in *Let the Children Come*, congregations can be in the forefront of educating their members about the problem, offering needed support and respite to parents feeling overwhelmed, and ensuring that their youngest members are assured a safe and nurturing environment.

Preventing child abuse is not simply a matter of *parents* doing a better job but rather it is about creating a context in which "doing better" is easier. As this book illustrates, congregations and people of faith can play an important role in fostering this type of personal transformation.

Communities of faith, by definition, foster a sense of interconnectedness and mutual reciprocity among their members. These relationships allow faith communities to promote a set of activities that underscore both the importance of *education* around the issue and *motivation* to accept personal responsibility for achieving the change we desire.

As sociologist Robert Wuthnow has noted, every volunteer effort or act of compassion finds its justification not in offering solutions for society's problems but in offering hope "both that the good society we envision is possible and that the very act of helping each other gives us strength and a common destiny."[5]

Enlightened public policy and publicly supported interventions are only part of what is needed to successfully combat child abuse. It remains important to remind the public that child abuse and neglect are serious threats to a child's healthy development and that overt violence toward children and a persistent lack of attention to their care and supervision is unacceptable.

Harder has offered every congregation a roadmap for fostering this type of change within its members and, potentially, within its community. Each person of faith has the ability to accept personal responsibility for reducing acts of child abuse and neglect by providing support to each other and offering protection to all children in the family, the congregation, and the community. Until the problem is owned by all individuals and all congregations, progress will be stymied and children will remain at risk.

—*Deborah Daro*
Chapin Hall at the University of Chicago

Preface

Children are hurt and killed every day through abuse and neglect. While the church would like to believe it doesn't happen here, research and experience tell us that it does. In the context of the Bible and faith, this book will help individual Christians and faith communities learn about their role in ending child abuse and neglect in all communities: church, home, extended family, neighborhood, school, and work. The book encourages Christians to consider the role they and their churches play in protecting children and strengthening families.

Let the Children Come is for Christians concerned about the safety and well-being of children. Church educators will use this book to lead adult Sunday school classes on the role of faith communities in ending child abuse and neglect. Church denominations will want to use this book to raise awareness and provide training on the prevention of child abuse and neglect.

Only a few books exist on the topic of child abuse and neglect as it relates to the church. Many books on the market speak primarily of sexual abuse and treatment of adult survivors of sexual abuse. Other books propose policies to protect the church against child abuse.

This book is unique in that it considers *all* types of child abuse and neglect, including neglect, physical abuse, emotional abuse, and sexual abuse. It is also unique in its wide-angle approach: members of our faith communities have a role in protecting children in all areas of life. This includes the church but also our homes, extended families, neighborhoods, schools, jobs, and more. Types of child abuse and neglect, statistics, and other material are presented for both the United States and Canada.

Each chapter contains real-life stories, discussion questions, and action items. The action items are suggested activities; they may not always be appropriate in your context. If unsure, seek the guidance of a pastor or other church leader. (If you have a history of hurting a child through abuse or neglect, please do not participate in activities that involve interaction with children.) Tips on teaching the material as well as sample prayers, exercises, frequently asked questions, and other resources are included as appendixes.

Several terms deserve an explanation: *Church* refers to the organized structure of a gathering of believers. *Faith community* is a looser term, referring to both individuals within a church and the collective gathering of the church. For purposes of this book, *church* and *faith community* are used interchangeably. I often use the phrase *the communities in which we live*. As humans, we exist in multiple communities: our family, our church, our extended family, our friends, our neighborhood, and our workplace. In this book, I argue that we have responsibility for the safekeeping of children in all these communities.

The phrase *end child abuse and neglect* can be seen as either provocative or prophetic. While I don't see the eradication of child abuse and neglect in my lifetime or yours, I do set it forth as a goal. A first step to achieving a better, safer world for our children is to envision a better, safer world for our children.

Quite often I refer to *our* children. Very seldom do I intend for us to think solely about the children in our families. Rather, in the collective sense, I think of all our children. As a society, we have responsibility for all children.

I also refer to *service providers*, referring to professionals in the community who work with or on behalf of children and families at risk for child abuse. They may be case managers, therapists, advocates, or policymakers, or they may carry other titles. Many service providers are also members of faith communities.

This book is full of stories. While most are based in real life, all names have been changed and situations altered. In some instances, individuals were notified that their story was used and their permission was received.

 You will find this hands graphic next to paragraphs that describe specific ways faith communities can work toward ending child abuse and neglect. New knowledge without subsequent changed behavior is insufficient. As we learn from James 2:17, "Faith by itself isn't enough. Unless it produces good deeds, it is dead and useless."

I have many, many people to thank for helping me complete this book. To gather background information, I engaged the services of three graduate social work students who interviewed faith community leaders from many Christian denominations. They interviewed in Nebraska and Iowa, in urban and rural settings. I wanted to know more about what faith communities saw as their role in preventing child abuse and neglect. To get a more balanced view, we also interviewed service providers who worked with child abuse and neglect, both faith-based and secular. Our findings identified strengths and opportunities for faith communities in preventing child abuse and neglect. Thank you for all your hours and hours of work: Erin O'Neill, Stephanie Huckins, and Jodi Gabel. I also thank all the church leaders and service providers who shared their thoughts, feelings, and beliefs with us.

Without the constant encouragement, prayers, and urgings of my dear friends and colleagues, Carol Knieriem and Mary Beth Hanus, I would never have brought this book to completion. Others also contributed through offering helpful information and feedback: Marlene Bogard, Linda Gehman Peachey, Elsie Goerzen, Jane Woelk, Julie Prey-Harbaugh, Kristina Haynie, and Tina Bartleson.

My thanks go to all the families whom I worked with over the years. By allowing me to walk with them for short spans of their lives, I was able to better appreciate the realities of life for those in poverty and without support. They provided me with the basis for many of the stories in this book.

My thanks extend especially to my brothers and sisters at First Mennonite Church in Lincoln, Nebraska. Marty Roth planted the idea for this project and, being the farmer that he is, continued to water and fertilize those seeds as this project grew to fruition. My pastor, David Orr, patiently provided insight into biblical passages that baffled me and offered incredibly helpful information and feedback.

Finally, my heartfelt thanks extend to my family. My husband, Stan, and our son, Jonathan, cheered me on each step of the way and allowed me to spend hours and hours on a project that seemed to never end. Thanks for standing by me. I will forever be grateful to my son's birthmother for giving me the opportunity to be a mom.

Introduction

Thanks be to God

Children are a delight. They make us smile. They bring us new life and adventures. They bring out the child in us as together we capture lightning bugs, toss water balloons, and blow bubbles. They remind us to appreciate the small and big things in our world. They ask questions that cause us to ponder life and faith in new ways.

Children are also a great responsibility. They are unbelievably vulnerable and sometimes lack common sense. They need us to protect them and provide their most basic and constant needs for food, shelter, clothing, and safety day in and day out, for many years. Children rely on us to get them medical care and education, to keep them away from hot burners, and to hold their hands when crossing the street. It is our responsibility as adults to care for children.

Sadly, scores of children are hurt everyday by those responsible to care for them. Some children are even killed by the people closest to them. This is hard for us to imagine; to be honest, we'd rather not think about it. But the reality is that children are being hurt. And these children have names. They have favorite ice cream flavors. They have gorgeous eyes. Through abuse and neglect, however, the light in these children's eyes is fading. They give up on the hope that someone will ever love them in a way that doesn't hurt. They need us to protect them, to value them, and to give them life again.

As Christians, we are committed to following Jesus' teachings. As recorded in Matthew 22:37-39, Jesus commands us to "Love the Lord your God with all your heart, all your soul, and all your mind." He goes on to command us to, "Love your neighbor as yourself." The children in our families, our churches, and the communities where we live and work are our "neighbors." We must do all we can to keep children safe. We must provide them with what they need to grow and thrive.

Until we are brave enough to face the reality of child abuse and neglect in our homes and communities, we may not recognize the child who needs protecting or the family who needs help. That four-year-old girl in your Sunday school class may not yet have the words or cognitive ability to explain that she is being hurt at home. She needs you to see the hints she is leaving for you: the withdrawal from normal classroom activities, bruises on her neck, toileting accidents, reluctance to go home. The eleven-month-old baby in the daycare where you work needs you to connect the dots and see that his chronic cough, his inability to sit by himself, and his dirty clothes are signs that his caretakers are not meeting his physical needs. The twelve-year-old girl who rides her bike on the sidewalk in front of your house every day needs you to befriend her so she can tell you about the things her stepbrother does to her in the middle of the night.

The purpose of this book is to help us, as individual Christians and faith communities, to protect children from abuse and neglect and to strengthen families. We will learn about the main types of child abuse, including neglect, emotional abuse, physical abuse, and sexual abuse. We will learn to recognize the signs and risk factors for abuse and neglect and consider our role in protecting children and strengthening families. From the context of the Bible and our faith, we will explore our role as Christians and the role that we and our churches can play in helping both children and families.

Some of us are adult survivors of abuse. We may still be hurting, we may be angry or confused, or we may avoid our feelings altogether. The purpose of this book is to prevent children from experiencing similar abuse or neglect. Reading this book may bring up emotions and memories for you. Seek the help of a professional counselor as you continue the healing journey. When you are ready, this book will give you the tools to help you protect the children in your communities.

Chapter 1

Dispelling Myths of Child Abuse and Neglect

Children are a gift from the LORD; they are a reward from him.
—Psalm 127:3

Child abuse and neglect is a problem of vast proportions. In the United States in 2008, more than 3.7 million children received an investigation or assessment from Child Protective Services (CPS). Of these children, more than 772,000 children (21 percent) were determined to have been victims of abuse and neglect.[1] (For the remainder, sufficient evidence was not available to substantiate abuse.) Similarly in Canada in 2003 (excluding Quebec), 217,319 child investigations were conducted, of which 103,297 (47 percent) were substantiated.[2]

Child abuse and neglect is a preventable tragedy. Even more alarming than the statistics already presented are the numerous situations of child abuse or neglect that are never reported, situations where safety is not provided and help is not there. These children are out of the reach of protection, and their families are not being given the help they need to provide a safe and healthy environment for children.

A first step toward ending child abuse and neglect is dispelling some of the myths around the subject and seeing how these myths help or hinder us from protecting the children in our churches and communities.

Myth 1: Since the Bible does not include the words *child abuse*, it does not have much to say on the subject. While the Bible does not include the exact words, *child abuse*, the Bible does have a lot to say about valuing children and providing for their needs. When you read the Bible through the lens of child abuse and neglect, you see many stories of children being either hurt or helped by their families. The Old Testament has numerous references to child sexual abuse—stories that startle and anger us. In the Gospels, we read that Jesus welcomed children. He even referred to children as examples for the rest of us. Such biblical passages will be explored in later chapters.

Myth 2: Child abuse occurs more frequently than child neglect. Abuse is an overt act by a parent or caregiver that brings harm to a child; neglect is the failure of a parent or caregiver to meet the needs of a child. Of the abuse and neglect reported to CPS in the United States in 2008 and substantiated, nearly three-fourths (71 percent) was for some type of neglect. The remainder of reports were for physical abuse (16 percent), sexual abuse (9 percent), emotional abuse (7 percent), medical neglect (2 percent) and other types of abuse or neglect (9 percent).[3] In Canada in 1998 (excluding Quebec), 25 percent of substantiated cases were for exposure to domestic violence, 25 percent for neglect, and 19 percent for physical abuse. Smaller proportions of cases were for emotional abuse (11 percent) and sexual abuse (2 percent). The remaining 18 percent were for multiple types of abuse or neglect.[4]

If we were to judge the prevalence of abuse and neglect from the headlines of our local newspapers, we would believe that sexual abuse and horrific cases of physical abuse occur the most often. Unless they are deemed especially heinous or malicious, cases of child neglect and physical abuse do not make the headlines. We must remember that just because the abuse stories are not broadcast on the media, hurting children are present in all our communities, and they need our help.

Myth 3: Children are more often abused by strangers than they are by people they know. It is important to teach children about *stranger danger*, but it is also important to realize that more children are hurt by their parents or other people they know and trust than by strangers. According to CPS records in the United States in 2008, more than 80 percent of perpetrators of abuse were the parents of the victim(s). And of the parental perpetrators, nearly all (90 percent) were the biological parents while 7 percent were other relatives.[5] According to Canadian police records, more than 80 percent of physical or sexual violence committed against children was perpetrated by someone known to the child. The offender most often was a friend or acquaintance (55 percent) or a family member (30 percent), followed by strangers (15 percent).[6] We must work to make our homes safe places for children.

If we were to look at child abductions, we would be surprised to see little call for *stranger danger* programs. According to the FBI's National Crime Information Center (NCIC) in 2007, 99 percent of reports on missing children in the United States classified the missing child as having run away; only 1 percent were classified as abducted by a non-custodial parent, and less than 1 percent were classified as having been abducted by a stranger.[7] Of course, a child abducted by a stranger is a horrific crime, but we must not neglect to protect our children from people they know.

Myth 4: Only a certain segment of the population has the potential to abuse children. Sadly, we all have the potential to hurt children. Those of us who are parents can probably understand how easy it might be to hurt children. When we get overwhelmed with the stresses of life, our children's normal antics may trigger a surprising response in us. We may lash out with words that we later wish we could take back. Our hands may reach out to strike the child before we can think to stop them. Sometimes, it is only by the grace of God that we do stop.

Some of us were fortunate to have grown up in families that did not hurt us. Some of us may not need to worry every day about how to provide shelter, food, and clothing for our children. Some of us may have a whole network of family and friends on whom we can call. Some of us may not be suffering from depression or from an addiction to alcohol, drugs, or gambling. If all of these are true of you: thanks be to God. Other families around you may not be so lucky. It is for the children in these families that we must be ready to help. Child abuse and neglect is not confined to any age, ethnicity, religion, or socioeconomic status.

Myth 5: Men do more abusing than women. Since women are more often the primary caretakers of children, they are more often the ones who abuse or neglect children. CPS records show that in the United States in 2008, some 56 percent of all confirmed perpetrators were female while 43 percent were male.[8] Men are more likely to be the perpetrators than women in two specific types of abuse: sexual abuse and a form of physical abuse called Shaken Baby Syndrome.

Myth 6: Parents who abuse or neglect their children do not care about their children. Parents who abuse or neglect their children usually do not wake up in the morning with the intention of hurting their children. In fact, offending parents usually care a lot about their children, but they lack the skills or resources to parent them effectively. Some parents lack healthy parenting skills, perhaps because they have never been modeled for them. Many parents lack knowledge of child development, and so have unrealistic expectations of their children.

For example, two-year-old José has a toileting accident while playing on the playground. His mother harshly punishes him for this offense, not realizing that a two-year-old who is engrossed in play cannot yet be expected to sense and respond to the subtle signs of the need to seek a rest room. Abusive parents are often isolated and do not have a grandmother, neighbor, or friend to turn to when they have concerns or need a break from parenting. Any addiction or mental illness can also seriously inhibit a parent's judgment in caring for a child.

Myth 7: All children who are abused will grow up to be abusers. It is true that perpetrators of abuse were often abused themselves as children. However, it is very important to note that just because someone suffered from abuse does not mean this person is doomed to repeat the cycle. Both research and experience show that the cycle of abuse can be broken.

Yolanda experienced harsh physical discipline from her stepmother throughout childhood. She has no fond memories of her stepmother; she has only memories of fear and dread. Now as a young mother herself, Yolanda is determined to be loving and kind toward her children. She is attending parenting classes and has talked extensively with a counselor about how she can break the cycle of abuse in her family.

Despite the brokenness of our pasts, we can raise children in a safe and healthy manner. We must come to terms with the reality that, especially when under pressure, we most easily resort to parenting the way we were parented. It is only with great effort, counseling, and support that we can break the cycle of abuse.

Myth 8: Abused children will usually discuss the abuse in an effort to stop it. Children are usually very reluctant to talk about abuse or neglect they are experiencing. The child may not realize that what he is experiencing is anything different from what other children experience. He may feel like the abuse is his fault, and if he would just be quieter, do better in school, or stop fighting with his brother, then his mother would not need to hit him. Perhaps the child doesn't want to get his parent in trouble, or he doesn't think anyone will believe him. For sexual abuse, in particular, offenders bind children to secrecy. The entire family may know, at some level, that the abuse is occurring, but this awareness is kept locked in a closet, hidden from public view.

I think of Jessica, a young girl whom my husband and I befriended. At the age of nine, Jessica had been sexually abused by her mother's boyfriend. Jessica and her little brothers had been removed from the home for a year before her mother was once again deemed to be able to protect and care for Jessica. During the time that Jessica was in foster care and after she returned home, my husband and I took her and her friends camping, out for ice cream, and to our home for simple times of being together.

After Jessica was returned to her mother, she would often disappear when it was time for us to take her home. We would eventually find her. But when we would pull in front of her house and she would see the car of her mother's new boyfriend, Jessica would duck behind the seat and beg us not to stop. I remember driving to a park with Jessica and walking around and around a pond, urging her to tell me why she was so afraid to go home. I suspected that Jessica was being sexually abused again, but despite my best efforts, she would not tell me.

Myth 9: All child injuries should be reported to authorities. Depending on the U.S. state in which we live, all adults are required by law to report child abuse. In every province and territory in Canada all adults are *mandated reporters* (with the exception of the Yukon Territory in which only professionals are mandated reporters of abuse). A mandated reporter must report suspected child abuse or neglect to the police or Child Protective Services (CPS). In turn, the police or CPS will conduct an investigation and initiate treatment and prosecution, if needed. Before making a report, we must consider the extent of the injury, the age of the child, and the child and/ or parent's explanation for the injury. For example, bruises on the elbows, knees, shins, or forehead of a preschooler are quite likely to be accidental. Children of this age are prone to falls and often bear the marks of these falls. However, injuries to a child's face, back, chest, stomach, or buttocks are much less likely to be accidental.

If a child has a broken arm and the parent claims she fell out of bed, we must be suspicious that the story does not match the injury. Also, if a child or parent's explanation of the injury changes from one day to the next, we must also be suspicious of an attempted cover-up and report the suspected abuse to CPS or the police. In no way should we investigate the suspected child abuse or neglect ourselves—leave that to the professionals.

Myth 10: It is the government's responsibility to respond to child abuse and neglect. Child abuse and neglect is such a huge and complex problem that no one entity can be held responsible for ending this tragedy. The government does play an important role in investigating reports of abuse, providing services, administering out-of-home care for victims, and prosecuting offenders. However, the government does not make a good parent. It does not have ears and eyes in every home and neighborhood or abundant resources to do all that we would hope it would do. Community agencies play a large role in preventing and responding to child abuse.

The church too can play a huge part in protecting children and strengthening families. Most child welfare agencies and workers welcome the opportunity to partner with a faith community. First, however, we as members of faith communities must accept the existence of the problem of child abuse and neglect, acknowledge our role, and become prepared to do our part.

When we close our eyes to the systemic problem of child abuse or look the other way when a child needs our help, we are not only perpetuating the problem, but giving our implicit blessing to the abuse and neglect of children.

As Christians and faith communities, we must acknowledge our vital role in ending the tragedy of child abuse and neglect. We must be brave enough to acknowledge this pervasive problem in our communities, and we must stand up on behalf of children. Just as our children cannot care for themselves, they cannot protect themselves. As Christians and faith communities, are we prepared to end child abuse and neglect?

Discussion Questions

1. What did you learn about child abuse and neglect in this chapter that surprised you?
2. What Bible passages come to mind about child abuse and neglect? (See Action Item 1 below.)
3. Do you think abuse by a parent hurts a child differently than abuse by a stranger? How and why?
4. Do you believe that we all have the potential to hurt children? What has been your experience?
5. What do you think someone who abuses or neglects a child looks like?
6. Do you think the cycle of abuse can be broken? Why or why not?
7. What can we do to end child abuse and neglect?

Action Items

1. Read any portion of the Bible through the lens of child abuse and neglect. Here are some places to start: Genesis 22, Genesis 37, Exodus 1–2, 1 Kings 3, Matthew 6.
2. Look through "For further reading" in the back of the book and note titles that may be interesting or helpful to you.
3. Call a parent, grandparent, teacher, youth pastor, or neighbor who influenced you in a positive way when you were a child. Thank that person.
4. Go to your community's yellow pages and find the section for *child abuse* or *family services*. What agencies are nearest your home, work, or church? Visit some of these places and pick up brochures to learn more about what they do.

Chapter 2

Spheres of Influence

One day as he saw the crowds gathering, Jesus went up on the mountainside and sat down. His disciples gathered around him and he began to teach them.

—*Matthew 5:1*

Jesus ministered to people in many places: along the shore, in the synagogues, on a mountainside, on a road, in a home, in a field, in a boat, on a hilltop, in an olive grove. We too encounter children nearly everywhere we go. We see them perched in grocery carts at the supermarket. We see them running and hear them screaming in our neighborhood playgrounds. We see them trudging to school in the early mornings, toting heavy backpacks. We see them suited up in brightly colored uniforms at soccer matches. And we see children in our Sunday school classrooms, fellowship halls, and sanctuaries.

Where does our responsibility to protect children from abuse and neglect begin, and where does it end? We work to protect the children in our own families. Is that enough? We also work to protect the children in our churches and in our extended families. Is that enough?

In this chapter, we will explore the communities in which we live and consider our role in protecting children in these places.

Church and children

As we know, church is much more than four walls and a roof. Church means a community of believers, a gathering of humans with a common purpose: to love God, neighbors, and self. Sure, we gather to benefit ourselves—through the giving and receiving of religious instruction, support, and encouragement—but we also gather to worship God and to serve others.

Some ways to measure a church's success is to count the number of people who attend a Sunday morning worship service or populate a church directory or pick up mail from church mailboxes. Other ways to measure the success of a church are less tangible, like the church's ability to be community. Being *community* means worshipping, learning, and serving together. It means supporting one another as well as celebrating, crying, and eating together.

Children are an important part of our church community. They have much to offer us, and they also require much of us. Children bring exuberant life and energy to our churches. They bring love, creativity, and skills. When we take the time to listen, children offer questions and insights that can baffle any theologian.

Children also require much of us. In church, we provide children with Sunday school teachers, children's stories, books, crafts, snacks, and playgrounds. For all that we provide for children, sometimes their presence disturbs us. How many times have you missed an announcement in church because a baby is crying? Have you wondered if the reason you have to keep getting the piano tuned is because children have been pounding on it? And what about having to repair that table in the toddler room because older kids have been dancing on it—for the third Sunday in a row! Or having to wash crayon off the wall in the preschool classroom?

Yes, while we enjoy the children in our churches, we also realize that they are a lot of work, and they require a lot of us. As adults, we also have the God-given responsibility to protect the children in our churches. Just as we must keep toddlers safe from poking sticks into outlets and school-aged children safe from climbing too high in a tree, so too we must do everything we can to protect the children in our churches from abuse and neglect.

Children are our most precious natural resource. They come to us as gifts from God, entrusted to our care for a short time. I can just imagine the twinkle in God's eye when he created baby Antoine, knowing that Antoine would one day play with his toy fish in the toilet. And I know God must have smiled the first time baby Alyssa giggled at her older sister's antics. God cares deeply about the children in our families and our churches, and so do we.

Children are our most precious natural resource.

Thinking bigger

What about the children who are not in our families or who do not come to our churches on Sunday morning? Do we have a responsibility to protect them from abuse and neglect too? I am reminded of the old finger play: "Here is the church. Here is the steeple. Open the doors and see all the people." But the people don't stay under the steeple all the time. Those of us who attend church also live in neighborhoods. We go to workplaces, visit friends, gather with extended family, volunteer at schools, and coach basketball teams. In addition to being a part of families and churches, we are also part of many other communities.

As faithful followers of Jesus, we strive to be Jesus' disciples everywhere we go, not just when we are in our church building. When we are at the park, at a baseball game, or at the grocery store, we are still followers of Christ. We must be prepared to protect children in all the places we encounter them.

Picture this: It's your birthday and your family has taken you to your favorite restaurant. You're enjoying pleasant conversation and warm breadsticks, eagerly anticipating the arrival of your food when your brain begins to register the sounds of a crying child. As the volume of the child's cries increases, so does your awareness of a man's raised voice. You automatically pre-sume the man is the father of the child. The exchange between child and father intensifies. As the child's cries turn to screams and kicks, the father's actions also become more harsh and animated. Captivated by the unfolding scene and yet trying to appear inconspicuous, you can't help but recognize that the father's anger is mounting. Your own pulse begins to quicken as you worry for the immedi-ate well-being of the child. Suddenly, the father harshly picks up the crying child and marches past your table toward the front door of the restaurant. You exchange glances with your spouse and . . . and . . . and what? Do you breathe a sigh of relief that the commotion is over and you can return to your cooling breadsticks? Do you say a prayer of thanksgiving that your fam-ily deals with conflict in a healthier manner? Do you remember how your own children acted when they were hungry and tired? Perhaps you wonder what happens to this child at home, out of the public eye. But do you *do* anything?

We must be prepared to protect children in all the places we encounter them.

When witnessing violence toward a child in public, we have several options. We can notify an authority—a restaurant manager, hotel clerk, or security guard—of our concerns. We can watch from a distance to see how things unfold, ready to intervene or report, if needed. We can offer under-standing and empathy to the parent in hopes of diffusing the anger. We can note the license plates on the offender's car and notify the police. None of these options are right all of the time, and sometimes the best option is to do nothing.

We must consider the age and level of vulnerability of the child. We must consider our own resources, including our abil-ity to confront an angry adult in such a way that does not bring harm to ourselves or greater harm to the child. We must consider the likelihood that we are misinterpreting the scene. Some children regularly exhibit behaviors that are physically explosive and present a risk to themselves or others, particularly children with ongoing mental health issues or disabilities. These children require a caretaker to act decisively and firmly.

But a child never deserves to be hurt in any way. Whatever we choose to do, we must acknowledge that involvement at any level requires some time, effort, and judgment on our part and some risk.

What is perhaps more problematic for us is when we have some level of relationship with the offending parent. The closer the relationship with the family, the more knowledge we have of the child's needs and behaviors as well as the actions and inactions of the parents. In our communities we must be the eyes that see the signs of abuse and neglect, and we must be the voice to speak out on behalf of the children. If not us, who? The closer we are to families, the more responsibility we have for the children, both for providing assistance and for reporting suspected abuse to authorities if needed.

I became suspicious when a five-year-old girl appeared in my front yard wanting to play with my child and me. When she showed up again the next day and again a few days later, I became more than curious and began to ask questions. I learned that not only was this child without adult supervision, but that she lived nearly a mile up the street. I walked her home and spoke with her mother, expressing my concern that her daughter was so far from home and without supervision. The mother's nonchalant response let me know that she was neither concerned nor would the behavior change. I made a phone call to Child Protective Services with my concerns. Yes, I was concerned that the mother would retaliate against me if she figured out where I lived, but I was much more concerned for her young daughter who was being allowed to walk the neighborhood without supervision—crossing streets and approaching strangers.

The decision-making process for that phone call to CPS was not as difficult as it may be when your eleven-year-old daughter comes home from school and tells you that her friend, Nancy, told her a secret. With some prodding, you learn that Nancy's eighteen-year-old stepbrother is coming into her bedroom at night and touching her private parts. You know Nancy's family well enough to know that they have had a very difficult year and that this stepbrother will soon be moving out of the house. What do you do? Do you hope that your daughter misunderstood her friend? Do you talk with Nancy or her mother? Do you call the authorities?

Remember the vulnerability of children; they need a voice, and that voice is yours.

These are the tougher decisions. You fear for harm to the child. You also struggle with your own denial. You worry for your future relationship with the family. We must remember the vulnerability of children. Often they don't know what is normal, they think abuse is their fault, and they certainly don't have the power to make it stop. They need a voice, and that voice is yours.

Involvement in community organizations

We are involved in many formal and informal organizations in our communities. When these organizations and agencies need volunteers, and they always do, the church is one of the first places they turn. Whether or not staff of these organizations and agencies attend church, they realize the compassion and desire to serve that is present in many of us who do. I have been to many meetings of community agencies and coalitions where questions were raised: "What about the faith community? How can we partner with them?"

Both as churches and as individual Christians, we have a lot to offer community organizations. As churches, we have outreach budgets and pews full of compassionate people. Churches and individuals can organize and contribute to food pantries and used clothing stores. Perhaps not often seen as child abuse prevention, reaching out with food, clothing, toys, and used furniture can positively impact a struggling family. While not causing neglect or abuse, poverty is a significant risk factor for child neglect and abuse. With its emphasis on sharing God's love and positive relationships, the church and its members can play a positive role in helping families within its own community as well as surrounding ones.

Unfortunately, community organizations are sometimes reluctant to turn to the church for help, and sometimes for good reason. Community organizations recognize that a church can be helpful and has good intentions, but community organizations question if a church will report suspected abuse. They fear that churches will try to handle situations themselves and get in over their heads and that unintentionally more children will get hurt. We will read more about this in later chapters.

As church members, we must be prepared to protect children and work to end child abuse, not just within the boundaries of our church property, but within our neighborhoods, schools, jobs, and everywhere else we step. What responsibility do we have for these children?

Discussion Questions

1. What qualities and challenges do children bring to your church? What do they require of your church?
2. Where was Jesus' church? What did he consider church?
3. Where was Jesus when he paid attention to children?
4. With paper and colored pencils draw a small circle in the center of the paper; put your name in the circle. Think back to the previous week. Draw more circles beside the center circle and identify each circle as a place you went (church, extended family, school, job, neighborhood, community organizations, sports, volunteer work).
   a. In how many of those places did you see children?
   b. How do you influence the children in each place?

Do they know you? Do you have a relationship with them?

c. What responsibility do you have for these children?

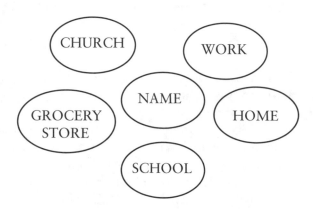

5. Share an experience where you worried about the welfare of a child. What did you observe? How did you feel? What did you do or not do and why?
6. What do you as a church have to offer in your communities (either as individuals or as the church as a whole)?
7. Why might the community be reluctant to ask for your help?

Action Items

1. Give a friendly greeting to children in your church this week. For children whom you don't know well, learn their names and activities they enjoy.
2. Look at your church's budget. How many lines are directly related to children? Would these lines be considered priorities by your church? How do you know? What percentage of the total budget contributes directly to the lives of children and families?

3. Take a walk in your neighborhood, and note how many children you see. Breathe a prayer for the safety and well-being of each child and caregiver.
4. Call a community agency that works with children and families. Ask for a list of their volunteer opportunities.

Chapter 3

What Does the Bible Say About Child Abuse and Neglect?

Anyone who welcomes a little child like this on my behalf is welcoming me.
—Matthew 18:5

Reading Scripture through the lens of child abuse and neglect, we learn about God's hopes for us in strengthening families and protecting children. We find stories of Jesus blessing and taking time for children. We find parents valuing and protecting their children. We find instructions for healthy family relationships. Overarching all of this, we find the importance of family and family relationships.

Although the word *child* occurs in the Bible 711 times and the word *children* occurs 521 times (*New Living Translation*), the phrase *child abuse* does not appear in English translations of the Bible. Nevertheless, the Bible is full of references to family relationships, like "son of God," "children of Israel" and "heavenly Father." The Bible frequently calls us into relationship with God and compares this relationship to those in our earthly families. Fortunately for us, God is a perfect parent.

Many of Jesus' healings responded to a parent's pleading on behalf of a son or daughter. The Bible never shows Jesus saying no to these parents. Instead, Jesus sets aside what he is doing, travels to the child's bedside, and heals the child. In the context of a culture where children were loved but socially powerless, Jesus' compassion for children was especially remarkable.

Throughout the Bible it really mattered what family you came from. Depending on who was in your family, you may have received a blessing, been banned from the community, or even been killed. Think of baby Moses. He was born into a Hebrew family, into the tribe of Levi. Because of this heritage Moses was condemned by Pharaoh to die (see Exodus 1, 2). That's a pretty steep penalty! Think of Ruth. Even though she was born a Moabite, she was welcomed into an Israelite family (see Ruth 1–4). Or think of David. He was born into the right family, wasn't he? As the youngest son of Jesse, he was chosen to be king of Israel (1 Samuel 16).

We must acknowledge that many of the blessings in our lives were not earned but rather bequeathed us by the grace of God.

We like to believe that our hard work and good choices have brought us to where we are. We must acknowledge, however, that many of our blessings were not earned but bequeathed us by the grace of God. The family into which I was born gave me a socioeconomic status, skin color, ethnicity, and geographic connection. I did not choose any of this. For both biblical and current times the families we are born into have a lot to do with directing our destiny.

In this chapter we will look at some scripture passages and see what they can teach us about child abuse and neglect and the role of faith communities. Throughout the Bible we read of families caring for one another, working together, and celebrating together. Old and New Testament passages alike challenge us to right relationships between parents and children. Some Scripture is relatively straightforward, easy to understand, and pleasing to our ears. Other passages are difficult to understand, confusing, even shocking. When interpreting Scripture, we must remember to consider the context and identify themes and patterns rather than isolating single verses.

Basic family relationships reflected in the Bible

Many biblical passages speak to the expectation that parents will seek to meet their children's needs. These passages can relate to child physical neglect, which is when a parent or caregiver fails to provide for a child's basic needs (food, clothing, shelter, or medical care) for reasons other than poverty.

Jesus' words in Matthew 6:25-30 beautifully illustrate God's love and care for us, God's children:

> "Look at the birds. They don't plant or harvest or store food in barns, for your heavenly Father feeds them. And aren't you far more valuable to him than they are? . . . And if God cares so wonderfully for wildflowers that are here today and thrown into the fire tomorrow, he will certainly care for you." (Matthew 6:26, 30)

God, cast as our heavenly Father, will meet the needs of his children. In the next chapter of Matthew, Jesus makes another basic assumption that a family will meet the needs of its offspring:

> You parents—if your children ask for a loaf of bread, do you give them a stone instead? Or if they ask for a fish, do you give them a snake? Of course not! So if you sinful people know how to give good gifts to your children, how much more will your heavenly Father give good gifts to those who ask him? (Matthew 7:9-11)

These scriptures point to the most basic assumption that parents will provide for the physical care of children. The care for children's spiritual, emotional, and intellectual needs is a natural progression. While 1 Timothy 5 gives instruction on care of widows, elders, and slaves, it doesn't mince words when it comes to caring for one's own family first: "But those who won't care for their relatives, especially in their own household, have denied the true faith. Such people are worse than unbelievers" (1 Timothy 5:8).

A nurturing parent places high priority on the care of her children. Recall the story in 1 Kings of two women who gave birth within a few days of each other. When one woman's baby died, she stole the other woman's baby; this resulted in a disagreement brought before the king. Hearing the story, King Solomon ruled that the baby should be cut in half. In this way each mother could have a part. Can you believe it? It's even more shocking to believe that one woman agreed to this deal! The baby's true mother, however, did not agree. She declared, "Give her the child—please do not kill him!" (1 Kings 3:26). The king thus determined she was the real mother, and the child was returned to her. In making his ruling, King Solomon relied on a parent's desire to seek the safety and well-being of her child first and foremost.

Other biblical passages further illustrate and provide guidelines for relationships between parents and children. While types of child abuse are not specifically mentioned, these passages provide insights as we consider the prevention of child abuse. The fifth of the Ten Commandments in Exodus 20:12 calls on children to honor their parents. Ephesians 6:1-2 and Colossians 3:20 echo this idea with commands for children to obey their parents. Similarly, in setting out requirements for church leaders, 1 Timothy 3 suggests that a father must "manage his own family well, having children who respect and obey him" (v. 4).

These commands for children to be obedient to their parents must not be interpreted as supportive of abuse. Each passage is balanced with other verses that speak to valuing children and respecting their rights as children of God. Both the Ephesians and Colossians passages urge fathers not to exasperate or embitter their children, but rather to encourage and train them in the ways of the Lord. Children never deserve to be hurt. They must be respected and valued as gifts from God.

Jesus values children

The words in Luke 18 draw one of my favorite pictures of Jesus. Parents have brought their young children to Jesus, hoping that he will touch and bless them. Imagine Jesus balancing a child on each knee with other children scrambling to sit on his lap. Parents stand close by, beaming from ear to ear as Jesus, the esteemed teacher, showers his attention on their precious children. Then Jesus' disciples storm in, grown men, beards flowing, all red in the face, shooing the children away. Can you hear them shouting, "Jesus has much more important things to tend to than a heap of children! Get them out of here! Go home!" Smiles fall from the children's faces as they slide off Jesus' lap and scurry back to their parents. Sad, disappointed faces are all around. Jesus rebukes his disciples and calls back the children: "Let the children come to me. Don't stop them! For the Kingdom of God belongs to those who are like these children. I tell you the truth, anyone who doesn't receive the Kingdom of God like a child will never enter it" (Luke 18:16b-17). Jesus gave families and disciples a strong message of his love and value for children that day.

Rather than being impatient with children's immaturity, as we so often are, Jesus urges his followers to become more child-like. Imagine that! Matthew 18:3-4 records Jesus' words: "Unless you turn from your sins and become like little children, you will never get into the Kingdom of Heaven. So anyone who becomes as humble as this little child is the greatest in the Kingdom of Heaven." When was the last time in your church that you held forth a child as a good example for the grown-ups?

Jesus also encourages us to welcome and protect children. "Anyone who welcomes a little child like this on my behalf is welcoming me" (Matthew 18:5). That is a powerful statement. It causes me to wonder about the ramifications of not welcoming a little child.

Nearly the harshest words ever recorded to have come from Jesus' mouth are addressed at anyone who causes a child to sin, saying that "it would be better for you to have a large millstone tied around your neck and be drowned in the depths of the sea" (v. 6). Jesus commands us not to "look down on any of these little ones" (v. 10).

Jesus encourages us to welcome and protect children.

He tells the beautiful story of a man with 100 sheep. Even though the shepherd has 99 of his sheep safe and accounted for, he is not happy until he has found the very last sheep. "In the same way, it is not my heavenly Father's will that even one of these little ones should perish" (v. 14).

One cannot read Matthew 18 without picking up on the high value Jesus placed on children. He recognized their vulnerability and need for care and protection. Even in a time and place in which children held low social status, Jesus respected their unique contributions and the examples they set for grown-ups. Can you imagine Jesus welcoming the children of your church? Gathering them onto his lap and preparing to tell them a story? How about the children in the community where you live? Can you imagine Jesus smiling at them and telling them that he loves them? I wonder how we can be Jesus to the children around us.

Mary and Joseph's parenting experience

I have often wondered what it must have been like for Mary and Joseph to parent a God-child. On one hand, Jesus was perfect. On the other, Jesus was growing and maturing as any young child. Did he not need direction and discipline? We are not given many clues into Jesus' life as a child, but the Luke 2 story of his family's trek home from Jerusalem stands out.

After celebrating the Feast of the Passover, the family begins the three-day journey to Nazareth. Jesus is presumably in with the crowd of family and friends returning home from the festivities. Large groups often traveled together, in part for protection against robbers and in part for company.

Whether it is a classic case of insufficient communication between parents, as each parent believes the child is with the other parent, or it's the case of an independent and happy child presumed to be spending carefree days with cousins and friends, we don't know. We do know that after a whole day of travel, Jesus is officially declared missing. A child is gone!

Imagine Mary and Joseph's growing realization that their son is not in the crowd and their shock of pain as they come to grips with his disappearance. It is conceivable, since Jesus was twelve years old, that Joseph thought Jesus was with the women and children in the front of the group, and Mary thought Jesus was with the old and young men in the back of the group.

In a panic the parents retrace their steps to Jerusalem and search for their son. An Amber Alert is not available for them.[1] Not until the third day after Jesus has gone missing is he located. And where is he? He is in the temple courts, speaking with the teachers of the law.

Joseph and Mary experience that agonizing mix of relief to have found their child and anger that he knowingly remained behind. Perhaps you can imagine Mary's tone of voice: "Son, why have you done this to us? Your father and I have been frantic, searching for you everywhere" (v. 48). And Jesus' adolescence shines through in his response: "Didn't you know I must be in my Father's house?" (v. 49). Scripture states that Joseph and Mary did not understand their son and that Jesus returned home with them and "was obedient to them" (v. 51).

Is this a case of neglectful supervision? After all, parents left a child behind. His whereabouts were unknown for three days. Who fed and sheltered him during these days? Was Jesus traumatized by the sights and sounds of the big city? Through the lens of our present-day society and culture, we gasp at the dangerousness of this situation and perhaps even at the irresponsibility of the parents. And yet, Jesus did not seem to have been harmed by this experience: he was resting in God's hands.

An example of poor parenting

Some Bible passages illustrate the mistreatment of children. In Matthew 14 we read of Herod Antipas and his wife exploiting their daughter sexually and causing her to play an active role in the violent killing of John the Baptist.

Herod and Herodias are illegally married, and John the Baptist has exposed their sin. The couple is angry with John to the point that they wish him dead. As ruler of the land, Herod has the capacity to have John executed. However, John is popular in Galilee, and since Herod fears the anger of the people, he has John imprisoned instead of killed.

As the story unfolds, Herod is enjoying himself at his birthday party. His wife's young daughter performs a dance that especially pleases him, and he offers to do anything that she requests. The young girl, a pawn in her mother's hands, asks for the head of John the Baptist on a tray. Herod then regrets his offer but succumbs to his daughter's wish. John is beheaded in prison. The daughter receives John's head on a tray and delivers it to her mother.

It doesn't take much imagination to assume the sexual nature of this girl's dance, nor the consumption of alcoholic drink and the power of showing off before Herod's friends. This daughter was not only encouraged to display her body in a sexual manner before adult males, she was used as a pawn in her parents' violent activities. In short, she was exposed to illicit adult activities before she was old enough to be able to make her own decisions about the wisdom of these types of activities. Additionally, as both a young person and a girl, she did not have the ability to say no to her parents. This girl was used inappropriately at the hands of her parents and likely had the course of her life shaped by these activities.

Care for orphans

The *New Living Translation* of the Bible uses the word *orphan* forty times. Nearly every reference commands the reader to care for the widows and orphans among them and condemns those who oppress widows and orphans. In Psalm 82:3 we read, "Give justice to the poor and the orphan; uphold the rights of the oppressed and the destitute."

In Isaiah 1:17: "Learn to do good. Seek justice. Help the oppressed. Defend the cause of orphans. Fight for the rights of widows." And in the New Testament: "Pure and genuine religion in the sight of God the Father means caring for orphans and widows in their distress and refusing to let the world corrupt you" (James 1:27).

Do you know any orphans? *Orphan* is not a word we use often. The word and the days of orphanages are behind us. While we may have retired these terms, the need has not gone away. The term *orphan* can be understood to mean any child who has lost a parent, either by death or divorce or any child who is in need of care or supervision. Now, do you know any orphans? I am quite sure you do.

We are unequivocally commanded to care for orphans and widows among us. God expects us to care for all children, especially those who are in need of family.

A child hurt

In the Old Testament in 2 Samuel 13 we find a disturbing story of sexual abuse within an incestuous family headed by King David, a man of great power. King David has many children by many women. One son is Amnon. Two other children by another woman are a son Absalom and a daughter Tamar.

In this story, Amnon and Absalom are adults and Tamar is a young girl. Amnon falls in love with his young stepsister, Tamar. Amnon works himself into a frenzy over his sexual desire for Tamar. He turns to his cousin Jonadab, and together they hatch a plan to entice Tamar into Amnon's clutches. Amnon pretends to be ill and asks his father (King David) to send Tamar to him so she can prepare him something to eat. Tamar obeys her father (he is the king after all!) and prepares bread in Amnon's presence.

As part of his plot, Amnon refuses to eat the bread until he is left alone with his sister. Amnon forcibly grabs his sister and demands that she come to bed with him. Tamar pleads for Amnon to stop. She speaks of the disgrace that will come upon them if Amnon continues with his plan. She even logically reminds Amnon that if he wants to marry her, all he has to do is ask his father (the king). Amnon refuses to listen to Tamar, overpowers her, and rapes her.

Immediately following the rape, Amnon's passion turns to intense hatred. He screams at Tamar, "Get out of here!" (v. 15). Again, Tamar, seeking to protect both of them, says, "Sending me away now is worse than what you've already done to me" (v. 16). Amnon refuses to listen to Tamar. He calls for his servant to put her out and bolt the door.

Tamar, beside herself with physical and emotional pain, tears her richly ornamented robe, worn to symbolize being the virgin daughter of the king. She puts ashes on her head and weeps aloud. Tamar's big brother, Absalom, notices Tamar and asks, "Is it true that Amnon has been with you? Well, my sister, keep quiet for now, since he's your brother. Don't you worry about it" (v. 20).

Tamar's account comes to an abrupt end; we are told that Tamar lives out her days in her brother Absalom's house as a desolate woman. The repercussions of this act of abuse reverberate throughout the family for years.

While Absalom and King David's anger toward Amnon and his actions unfolds in 2 Samuel, justice is never accomplished, and healing and wholeness are not brought to Tamar nor to her family. Although the anger of both Absalom and King David are recorded in the Scriptures, it appears that neither of them spoke directly to Amnon, nor does it appear they told the truth to others in the family or community. Some suggest that King David did not punish his son, Amnon, because he loved him and because he was his firstborn.

Parallel to his brother's evil plot, Absalom devises and carries out an elaborate plan to trap and kill his brother, Amnon. King David greatly mourns his oldest son's death. He later desires a relationship with Absalom, but the father-son relationship is never fully restored. Absalom's anger consumes him, and he attempts to usurp David from his throne but is killed in the process.

What a tragic story of power and greed! What total disregard for the needs, thoughts, and feelings of others, especially of Tamar. Despite her pleas for him to stop, Tamar was overpowered by her attacker. Amnon committed a gross sin when he so totally and unrelentingly violated his stepsister. He devastated her physically, emotionally, and socially. He stole her virginity, her hopes for marriage and children. This one act of violence and lust caused Tamar, the victim, to carry a badge of dishonor the rest of her life.

Explicitly or not, many people share the guilt for the sexual abuse of Tamar: Amnon's cousin who helped hatch the plan; King David who sent his daughter to Amnon; the servants who were present, left the room, and bolted the door; perhaps even Absalom. It appears Amnon had a reputation for these types of escapades. Upon seeing Tamar with her robes torn, Absalom assumed that she had been attacked by Amnon. Could not Absalom have protected Tamar? Absalom unwittingly contributed to Tamar's pain by hiding her in his home and passive-aggressively seeking revenge on Amnon.

The story of the sexual abuse of Tamar has many parallels to our current knowledge and experience of sexual abuse. We see the offender's desire for power and control over the victim and the offender's meticulous efforts to devise a plan to trap the victim. We see other ways in which power, authority, and culture worked against this young girl whose father demanded that she serve her brother.

Tamar's desires and thoughts are not considered by any of the parties to this tragic drama. She is not given a choice when told to wait on her ailing brother. Her repeated objections are not heard by Amnon as he attacks her. Even when Tamar's brother steps in as her alleged rescuer, we do not hear Tamar's thoughts and feelings expressed or considered. And finally, the secrecy that so often engulfs sexual abuse is evidenced in this story. Tamar is whisked off into her brother's house as if she is the one to blame. Too often today victims are told to "get over it." The family is divided by this elephant in the living room and sides literally war against one another in an unhealthy thirst for vengeance that ends in death.

The Bible is full of good and bad examples of families caring for their children. We are reminded of Jesus' greatest commandment to love our neighbors as ourselves in Matthew 22:37-39, and we remember that children are our neighbors and need care and protection. In later chapters we will consider other biblical passages and examples.

Discussion Questions

1. Jesus was willing to take time for children. When is it the easiest for you to take time for children? When is it the hardest?
2. What childlike characteristics do you think Jesus was praising in Matthew 18?
3. How might these verses apply to child abuse and neglect? "If a man has a hundred sheep and one of them wanders away, what will he do? Won't he leave the ninety-nine others on the hills and go out to search for the one that is lost? And if he finds it, I tell you the truth, he will rejoice over it more than over the ninety-nine that didn't wander away! In the same way, it is not my heavenly Father's will that even one of these little ones should perish" (Matthew 18:12-14).

4. What strengths do you identify in Jesus' family? What do you think of the parenting skills exhibited by Joseph and Mary during their trip to and from Jerusalem, as recorded in Luke 2:41-52?
5. With which character in the story of Tamar are you the most angry? Who should have done something to stop this from happening? Was Tamar partly to blame? Why or why not?
6. How has the family you were born into directed your destiny?

Action Items

1. Read the book of Matthew and note the references to children. Now read a newspaper and again note the references to children. What do you discover about the status and role of children in each of these settings?
2. Consider the children in your life. What good qualities do they possess that you could learn from?
3. Make a list of *orphans* you know. What could you do to improve the lives of these children?
4. Read 2 Samuel 13–24. Reflect on the role of each character: what was the contribution of each to the safety of Tamar or the strength of her family?
5. Write down the names of children and families in your community. Pray regularly for the safety and well-being of each one.

Chapter 4

Child Abuse and Neglect 101

You parents—if your children ask for a loaf of bread, do you give them a stone instead? Or if they ask for a fish, do you give them a snake? Of course not!

—Matthew 7:9-10

In the best of times, young people date, get married, have children, and live together happily ever after. In reality, life doesn't always happen that way. Families come in all shapes and sizes; they always have and they always will. Grandparents raise their grandchildren. Single mothers struggle to provide care and supervision for their children while holding down two or more jobs. Blended families come in as many constellations as there are stars in the sky.

The traditional family of two parents and two-and-a-half children, with the father at the office, mom at home, a white picket fence, two cars in the garage, and a pet dog named Spot is a mirage. Perhaps it's not even one that we wish to attain.

Our families must meet the needs of each member. If the times are good and mental health runs high, each member of the family, young or old, can make his unique contribution and in return can have his needs met for food, shelter, and love. Some families are able to pass strengths such as meaningful religious traditions, economic stability, and high educational values from generation to generation. Many families, however, struggle to find positive parenting models and to make ends meet.

51

It is for the children in all of these families that we must work together to end child abuse and neglect. Whether one is a concerned individual, a responsible community member, a church member, or a government worker, each plays a role. There is more than enough work for all of us. Increasing our awareness and knowledge of child abuse and neglect is critical if we are going to stand together and bring an end to it. This chapter contains basic information on child abuse and neglect. Subsequent chapters will discuss specific types of child abuse and neglect.

History of child abuse and neglect

Child abuse can be traced back to the earliest days of history. Long ago children were considered mere possessions of their parents, often of just their father. Parents would make life-and-death decisions as basic as which baby could live and which baby could not, often depending on the child's gender or a physical trait.

In our not-too-distant history, many children in North America were valued only for their ability to provide labor and other economic incentive. It wasn't until the late nineteenth century that the U.S. government began to take some responsibility for the care of children when the parents could not or would not provide adequate care.

In 1912 the U.S. government established the Children's Bureau, but it was not until 1974 that Americans passed their first major federal policy around child welfare: the Child Abuse Prevention and Treatment Act (CAPTA). This act provided a basic definition for child abuse and neglect, a means for identifying child victims, and procedures for reporting suspected child abuse and neglect.

According to CAPTA, child abuse and neglect is, at a minimum: "Any recent act or failure to act on the part of a parent or caretaker which results in death, serious physical or emotional harm, sexual abuse or exploitation; or an act or failure to act which presents an imminent risk of serious harm."[1]

While this federal act provides the minimum standards,

each state is responsible for providing its own definitions of child abuse and neglect and its own procedures for reporting suspected child abuse and neglect.

In Canada, the province of Ontario was the first to pass legislation: the Child Protection Act in 1893, with most other provinces following suit by 1901. The first Children's Aid Society was established in Toronto in 1891, and by 1912 five more were established across Ontario.[2] Provinces and territories began passing mandatory reporting laws in the 1960s.[3] The passing of the landmark Child and Family Services Act in 1984 accomplished three things: professionalization of the service system, emphasis on the province government's responsibility for delivery of child welfare services, and a shift to non-institutional prevention-oriented services. In 2007 the Supreme Court of Canada reaffirmed the mandate of Children's Aid Societies under the Child and Family Services Act to act in the best interests of the child, to protect children and youth from abuse and neglect and to ensure their well-being.[4]

Child abuse and neglect today

In the United States the Child Welfare Information Gateway contains more information and statistics on child abuse and neglect in the United States than you could ever dream of. This clearinghouse of information can be easily found at www.childwelfare.gov. The Child Welfare Information Gateway was created out of the United States Department of Health and Human Services and provides access to electronic and print publications on all areas of child welfare.

The counterpart in Canada is the National Clearinghouse on Family Violence (NCFV), administered through the Public Health Agency of Canada through its Family Violence Initiative. The NCFV collects, develops, and disseminates resources on prevention, protection, and treatment in both English and French. This Canadian clearinghouse can be found at www.phac aspc.gc.ca/ncfv-cnivf.

A particularly helpful document found on the Child Welfare Information Gateway site (United States) is titled, "A Coordinated Response to Child Abuse and Neglect: The Foundation for Practice" (Goldman and Wolcott, 2003). This manual lists and discusses the following philosophical tenets that underlie sound practices in community responses to child abuse and neglect. They are:

- Prevention programs are necessary to strengthen families and reduce the likelihood of child abuse and neglect.
- The responsibility for addressing child maltreatment is shared among community professionals and citizens.
- A safe and permanent home is the best place for a child to grow up.
- When parents (or caregivers) are unable or unwilling to fulfill their responsibilities to provide adequate care and to keep their children safe, CPS (Child Protective Services) has the mandate to intervene.
- Most parents want to be good parents and have the strength and capacity, when adequately supported, to care for their children and keep them safe.
- To help families protect their children and meet their basic needs, the community's response must demonstrate respect for every person involved.
- Services must be individualized and tailored.
- Child protection and service delivery approaches should be family centered.
- Interventions need to be sensitive to the cultures, beliefs, and customs of all families.
- To best protect a child's overall well-being, agencies must assure that children move to permanency as quickly as possible.[5]

Children of all ages are abused and neglected. Tragically, young children are disproportionately represented among the victims. In 2008 in the United States, nearly one-third (33 percent) of all victims of child abuse were younger than four years old. Girls of all ages are slightly more likely to be victimized than are boys.[6] In 2003 in Canada, 22 percent of all victims were younger than four years old, and boys were slightly more likely to be victimized than girls.[7]

In 2008, some 794,000 children were victims of maltreatment in the United States; that is 10.3 per 1,000 children. An estimated 3.7 million children received an assessment or investigation from CPS, meaning they were likely at risk for abuse or neglect. According to police records in Canada, 13,200 children and youth were victims of physical or sexual assault at the hands of a family member in 2007.[8] Children of minority races are over-represented in child welfare systems[9]; of particular concern in Canada are children from Aboriginal families, and in the United States children from African-American families.[10]

As shown in this graph, nearly three-fourths of child victims in the United States suffer from neglect. Much smaller proportions of children suffer from all other types of abuse and neglect.[11] It may surprise you that nearly one-third (32 percent)

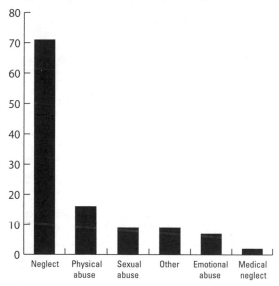

Types of Child Abuse by Percentage of Victims

Child Fatalities and Types of Abuse

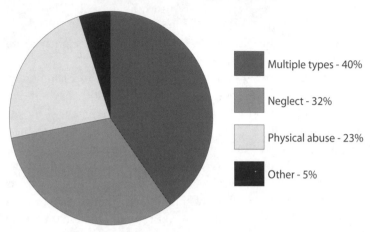

Multiple types - 40%

Neglect - 32%

Physical abuse - 23%

Other - 5%

of child abuse fatalities in 2008 in the United States were from neglect.[12]

Children in faith communities are not immune from child abuse. Among members of Mennonite Church USA congregations in 2006, 21 percent of women and 6 percent of men reported being sexually abused or violated at some time in their life; 12 percent of women and 4 percent of men reported that they received this abuse as a child.[13]

Similar statistics were reported in a survey conducted 20 years ago among Canadian Mennonites, where 27 percent of females and 15 percent of males reported having been sexually abused prior to the age of 18 years.[14] Likewise, a study by the Christian Reformed Church nearly 20 years ago found that 28 percent of adult members had been victims of abuse or neglect as children.[15]

The statistics do not matter to the individual child who is being victimized. What matters to the child is being kept safe and being helped when help is needed. We must work to stop all types of abuse and neglect from hurting any of our children and families.

An international perspective

Parents, churches, and governments around the world care about children. Unfortunately, children everywhere suffer abuse and neglect as well as violence, exploitation, and discrimination. While child protection violations are hard to measure amidst differing social norms and political systems, according to UNICEF's publication, *State of the World's Children*, "Violence may affect between 500 million and 1.5 billion children, and an estimated 150 million children, ages 5–14, are engaged in child labor. More than 70 million women and girls, ages 15–49, in twenty-nine countries have been subjected to female genital mutilation/cutting."[16]

> The statistics do not matter to the individual child who is being victimized. What matters to the child is being kept safe and being helped when help is needed.

Identifying and protecting children at risk for abuse and neglect is a common goal, with most countries recognizing physical and sexual abuse as detrimental to children. Indeed, a survey by the International Society for the Prevention of Child Abuse and Neglect found that 90 percent of responding countries had official child maltreatment policies. As we would expect, children in countries facing extreme economic hardship and social disruption are at particular risk,[17] but that does not let us off the hook in North America.

UNICEF conducted a study titled, "An Overview of Child Well-being in Rich Countries" examining six dimensions of child well-being. Of the twenty-one nations assessed, Canada ranked twelfth and the United States ranked twentieth—or second from last—in overall child well-being. On the dimension of *health and safety* for children, Canada ranked thirteenth and the United States ranked twenty-first. On the dimension of *family and peer relationships*, Canada ranked eighteenth and the United States ranked twentieth.[18] Clearly, we have a lot to accomplish at national and local levels for the sake of our children.

The United Nations adopted an international treaty in 1989 titled, "Convention on the Rights of the Child." This treaty celebrates the rights of children, including special protection and access to education and healthcare. The treaty recognizes that each child, "for the full and harmonious development of his or her personality, should grow up in a family environment, in an atmosphere of happiness, love and understanding."[19] This treaty is the most widely ratified human rights treaty in history.[20]

Consequences of child abuse and neglect

Child abuse and neglect have dire consequences for the child, family, church, and society. The child victim suffers physically, emotionally, behaviorally, and spiritually. The family is affected forever. If involved, the church reels from what has happened and must consider its role. And society pays in many ways and through many systems: child welfare, the police and legal systems, as well as healthcare which includes mental health programs.

The effects of child abuse and neglect on a child depend on many factors, including the child's age and developmental level when the abuse or neglect occurred; the type of abuse suffered; the frequency, duration, and severity of the abuse; and the relationship between the victim and the abuser.[21] Some of the effects of abuse and neglect are a direct result of injury inflicted; other effects are a result of not having positive interactions with a parent or not having basic physical and emotional needs met.

Physical injuries such as broken bones, cuts, and bruises are easily identified. Other physical injuries include impaired brain development, particularly in babies and young children, as well as poor physical health and sexually transmitted diseases.

The emotional effects of child abuse and neglect are vast. Being victimized by child abuse and neglect often causes a child to feel isolated and depressed. She may experience difficulty in social relationships, not want to trust anyone, and develop an attachment disorder.

Child victims also frequently suffer cognitively; language development may be delayed in younger children and academic achievement may be stunted in school-aged children. Adolescents who have suffered abuse or neglect are much more likely to get in trouble with the law and to abuse alcohol or drugs.

Society also bears the effects of child abuse and neglect as it must pour resources into systems of child welfare, law enforcement, health and mental health systems to respond to the needs of children and families. The indirect costs to society are immense and impossible to fathom; they include costs for crime and imprisonment, *The consequences of child abuse and neglect are far-reaching and impossible to quantify.* health and mental healthcare, treatment for domestic violence and substance abuse, and loss of productivity at work.[22]

The consequences of child abuse and neglect are far-reaching and impossible to quantify. We must do all we can to stop abuse and neglect from happening in the first place. The efforts we put into prevention can truly make a world of difference for a child. To prevent the tragedy of child abuse and neglect, we must first understand the various types of child abuse and neglect.

In the following chapters, four broad types of abuse and neglect will be defined and described: neglect, emotional abuse, physical abuse, and sexual abuse. We will learn about the effects on children and how to recognize each type of abuse or neglect. Most importantly, we will begin our discussion of what we can do to end each type of abuse and neglect.

Discussion Questions

1. If there was such a thing as a perfect family, what would it look and act like?
2. What do you know about the definition for child abuse in your state or province?
3. What do you know about the prevalence of child abuse and neglect in your community?

4. Which of the philosophical tenets set forth by Goldman and Wolcott (2003) do you or your faith community support? In which tenets do you see the faith community playing a role?
5. As you think about your own family history, what actions (or inactions) were acceptable twenty to fifty years ago but would be called child abuse or neglect today? How do you account for this change?

Action Items

1. In the United States, explore the Child Welfare Information Gateway website: www.childwelfare.gov. Find information (definitions, statistics) specific to your state. In Canada, explore the National Clearinghouse on Family Violence, Public Health Agency of Canada website: www.phac-aspc.gc.ca/ncfv-cnivf.
2. Read the Convention on the Rights of the Child from the United Nations (www2.ohchr.org/english/law/crc.htm). Discuss reasons why a country may or may not want to ratify this treaty.
3. Invite a child welfare professional from your community to talk with your class or group. Find out what you can do to make a positive difference for children and families in your community.

Chapter 5

A Look at Neglect and Emotional Abuse

Kind words are like honey—sweet to the soul and healthy for the body.
—Proverbs 16:24

Of all types of child abuse, neglect occurs the most often. In general, neglect is the failure to provide for a child's basic needs, and it may involve physical, medical, educational, or emotional neglect. In Canada, neglect is generally defined in this way: "The child has suffered harm or the child's safety or development has been endangered as a result of the caregiver(s)' failure to provide for or protect the child."[1] You can imagine how long-term malnutrition, lack of medical care, inattention to education, and emotional deprivation can seriously harm a child.

Two types of neglect:

- Physical neglect
- Neglectful supervision

Physical neglect

The broad category of neglect that involves by far the most child victims is physical neglect. Physical neglect involves the failure of a caretaker to provide necessary food or shelter or appropriate supervision.[2] A neglected child may be chronically hungry, dressed inappropriately, and often dirty or sick.

Remember that day you sent your child to school without a jacket because you hadn't known a cold front was coming through? While perhaps causing your child to shiver all the way home from school, this would not be classified as neglect. Neglect is consistently sending your child to school without a coat on cold winter days. Like other types of abuse, physical neglect is a pattern of action or inaction that brings harm to a child.

When I think of neglect, the picture of nine-month-old Savannah flashes into my mind. This was the first time I had looked neglect in the face, and the image will stay with me for the rest of my life. Savannah's mother, Ruth, was 18 years old. She was a single mother who had dropped out of school when she became pregnant. Savannah was dirty every time I saw her: her clothes were dirty, her skin was dirty, and her diaper was so full that it would nearly fall off as she crawled across the filthy floor. To her credit, Ruth had a high chair for Savannah; unfortunately, the entire high chair was caked with old food. The tray appeared as though it had not been cleaned in weeks.

Every time I visited the home, there was a different man sleeping on the couch. I suspected drug use. When Savannah became ill and I could not convince Ruth to seek medical care for her, I had to report Ruth to CPS for neglect. As a community worker, I had tried to provide all the tools for Ruth to provide better care for her child and herself, but Ruth did not make use of these tools. I could not wait for Ruth to get her act together; her child's very basic well-being was at stake. CPS removed Savannah from her mother's care and placed her in foster care.

Savannah's family had many of the risk factors for neglect. Her mother was unmarried, young, poor, and a high school dropout. Ruth was indiscriminately allowing men access to her life and apartment, and consequently, access to her baby girl. Ruth may have been abusing drugs or alcohol. None of these factors are identified as singular causes for neglect, but, put together into one package, they are a recipe for disaster for children.

Physical neglect includes the deprivation of food, clothing, shelter, or medical care for reasons other than poverty. Poverty is a risk factor for neglect: "Children from families with incomes less than $15,000 a year, compared to children from families with incomes greater than $30,000 a year are 22 times more likely to experience some form of maltreatment, and 44 times more likely to be victims of neglect."[3] Nevertheless, most poor families do not neglect their children.

Most parents of poor families do all they can to meet the needs of their children even if that means adults in the family must do without. Most parents of poor families work extremely hard, carefully budgeting their meager income. The difference is that neglectful parents are not able to consider the needs of their children. They may lack empathy. They may be too strung out on drugs to notice. They may live in constant fear of personal or community violence.

I know I am in a neglectful home when I see large-screen TVs or other expensive items but the baby is without diapers and the children are without clothing and food. I think of the family who lived in an upscale, three-level brick home and was planning a three-week trip to Disney World and yet could not buy their children clothing or supplies for school.

Neglectful supervision

Neglectful supervision puts many children at risk every day. Families often struggle with knowing when they can leave their child home alone safely. The law does not stipulate a specific age when a child can be left alone because of the many factors to consider: maturity of the child, safety of the home and neighborhood, and other children in the home.

I think of twenty-four-year-old Eva. Her husband was in jail, and she was left to care for her aging mother and three children under the age of six. Eva needed and wanted to work to support her family. Because of her minimal skills and education, few jobs were open to her. The minimum-wage job she had did not provide her with a flexible schedule or help with childcare. Eva had to catch the bus to work, which took additional time out of her day.

At first, Eva's mother was able to care for the children. But when the police found the children home alone and the grandmother wandering the neighborhood, Eva had to come to grips with the reality that her mother's advancing case of Alzheimer's no longer allowed her to be an adequate caretaker for the children. Eva set up daycare, but she did not know what to do on days when school was cancelled unexpectedly or a child was ill. She had left her children home alone so many times before, and nothing bad had happened. Would it hurt to do it just one more time? If she didn't show up for work, she might lose her job. She needed this next paycheck to pay her rent and to buy her son the pair of shoes he needed.

One day at work, Eva received a phone call from an ambulance crew that had been called to her apartment. A neighbor had heard a huge crash and then children screaming. Eva's six-year-old son had climbed up on a cabinet to reach for the remote. In the process, he had pulled the cabinet and the TV down on himself. The ambulance crew had to lift the furniture off him and take him to the hospital where he was treated for a broken arm. Thanks to the referral to CPS, Eva received more adequate daycare, a referral to an adult day center for her mother, and a mentor to help her learn about appropriate expectations of children and information on healthy parenting skills.

Unfortunately, the current welfare law exacerbates supervision problems for many poor families: it emphasizes employment for parents but does not often provide sufficient funds for quality daycare. A minimum-wage job is not enough money for a family to pay for childcare as parents also struggle to pay for housing, food, and healthcare. Ironically, most parents earning a minimum wage make too much money to receive government assistance for their childcare, and yet they do not earn enough money to pay for quality care for their children in addition to all their other expenses.

A pattern of neglectful supervision is particularly hard to change because typically a parent has successfully left the children home alone in the past, so the parent believes he or she is immune from problems in the future. Unfortunately, children do not have the judgment to keep themselves safe at home alone.

Eight-year-old Jackson found a cigarette lighter in the attic. He flicked it on, and the little flame fascinated him. Before he knew it, the pile of newspapers next to him was on fire, and then the whole attic was engulfed in flames. Jackson escaped the fire, but his younger brother and sisters did not. Now that Jackson is older, he lives with the guilt of knowing he started the fire that killed his siblings. And his mother must live with the guilt of knowing that she should have been home to protect her children.

I think of Leticia who wanted to pick something up from a friend's house. Leticia's ten-month-old daughter, Marie, was asleep on the couch, and Leticia thought she would be gone only for a few moments. While Leticia was gone, Marie woke up and crawled into the bathroom. Marie pulled up to the toilet and dropped a toy in. She then toppled into the toilet head-first while trying to retrieve the toy. Unfortunately, by the time Leticia returned home, Marie had drowned and was not able to be resuscitated by rescue workers. Leticia learned the hard way about the importance of constant supervision of children as well as the importance of making a child's living area safe.

I also think of six-month-old twins, José and Gerald, whose mother took them with her to the bar. In the wee hours of the night, the babies were left in the care of someone the mother had just met while she went off with her boyfriend. The babies were found abandoned in the bar's parking lot. The mother admitted to the police that she did not know the name of the person with whom she had hastily left her babies.

Our response to neglect

 In my experience, neglect is one of the most difficult types of abuse to confront and change. To truly help a family and bring them to wholeness, we must build a relationship with the family and come to a good understanding of their context and needs.

We can provide cleaning supplies, but unless a family knows how to use them and does, we have not been effective in stopping the neglect of the children in the home. We may need to talk with a parent about the importance of keeping a clean floor while her child is learning to crawl. We may need to educate a parent about germs—how they can cause a child to become ill and what the parent can do to protect the children. We may need to teach the parent about nutrition and help her shop for food items that

Neglect is one of the most difficult types of abuse to confront and change.

are both inexpensive and nutritious (and ones her kids will eat!). We may need to teach the parent about child development and help her to see that her baby needs to be picked up, held, and talked to. We may need to teach the parent that a baby does not cry because he is mean or does not like his parent but because that is the only way he has to communicate that he is hungry, bored, in pain, or needing a diaper change. We must work to understand the underlying causes for neglect and be creative, flexible, and respectful in our responses.

While the Bible may not forthrightly state, "Thou shalt not neglect your children," it does expect that we will work to meet the needs of our family (Matthew 6–7).

Reading Genesis causes us to wonder about the parenting capacities of Abraham and Sarah. Much to their dismay, Abraham and Sarah are without offspring. Sarah hatches a plan to remedy the situation and sends her servant to lie with Abraham.

The plan backfires when Sarah later becomes jealous of her servant and stepson. Could it be that a lack of parenting experience allowed Abraham and Sarah to banish Hagar and young Ishmael to the wilderness with no provisions for their shelter and only a small amount of water and food? In her desperation, Hagar lays Ishmael under a bush and steps aside so she will not have to watch him die. Fortunately, God provides for the needs of Hagar and her young son.

> We must work to understand the underlying causes for the neglect and be creative, flexible, and respectful in our responses.

Banishing Hagar and Ishmael to the wilderness seems like odd behavior for the parents of a long-awaited son. But perhaps it is indicative of the parents' guilt after overriding God's promise for a son and finding their own way.

We must not minimize the seriousness of neglect. We must work on both the individual and community levels to help families get what they need to keep their children safe. If you suspect a child is being neglected, please make a report to CPS or the police as soon as possible: you can make the difference for a child.

Emotional abuse

Emotional abuse is nearly as difficult to define as it is to prove. The emotional abuse of a child does not usually leave a mark that can be measured or captured in a photograph. Nevertheless, emotional abuse scars the hearts and minds of our children in ways that are not easily healed. Emotional abuse may include continual scapegoating, rejection, or exposure to violence by a child's parent or caretaker. Emotional abuse may also include a parent's failure to let a child know that she is loved, wanted, secure, and worthy. When this is the pattern, a child's ability to form healthy relationships with God, self, and others is impaired.

Emotional abuse takes many forms and is most harmful when it occurs as a repeated pattern of behavior. One type of emotional abuse is spurning. In this type of abuse, the child is belittled, degraded, shamed, ridiculed, and/or publicly humiliated by a parent. Words said to or about our children in their presence leave a mark on their psyche that isn't easily erased. Emotional abuse erodes a child's fragile sense of self and instills a sense of inadequacy and fear.

Another type of emotional abuse is terrorizing, which occurs when a parent threatens to hurt, abandon, or even kill a child. Depending on the developmental level of the child, words and threats are perceived literally. When a parent tells a child, "You're just like Uncle Joe. You're certainly as lazy as he is!" the child may go to the mirror and expect to begin to take on the physical characteristics of Uncle Joe. When a parent threatens to leave a child at the police station if the child disobeys again, he develops a fear of not only the police station but also of the parent. Additionally, emotional abuse may negatively skew the child's image of individuals who may actually be in a position to help.

I recently witnessed a child stub her toe and run to her parent for help. Rather than providing comfort, the mother declared, "Let's go to the doctor! He'll cut your foot off!" Not surprisingly, the child's face registered shock, and she turned and ran back to play. The parent was overheard laughing and saying to herself, "That took care of it! Now she won't come crying back to me every time she gets hurt."

In isolation, this scene may not be concerning to you. However, when this type of harsh response is given repeatedly, the child will certainly learn that the parent is not there to offer protection or comfort. In this instance, the child also develops a skewed image of a medical doctor that will make her quite fearful when medical attention or an appointment is actually required. The parent has not only hurt the child, but also cheated herself out of a loving, reciprocal relationship with her child. All it would have taken was a quick look at the toe, a kiss on the head, and the child would have happily returned to play without being any worse for the wear.

Isolating a child can be another form of emotional abuse. In this instance, a parent places unreasonable limitations on a child's activities or expressions. I have met families who do not allow their children to engage in any normal activities, such as playing outside or on a playground, making friends, or engaging in sports or other extracurricular activities. That said, I am certainly in favor of setting reasonable boundaries for our children, especially when we do so in consideration of their safety, well-being, or our resources.

Emotional abuse comes into the picture when a child is not allowed to engage in any normal age-appropriate activities. This child, if allowed to go to school, must always come straight home and is instructed to never, ever play or even speak with another child. Phone calls, emails, texting are all strictly prohibited. A child who is isolated in such a fashion develops an unhealthy fear of the world and is unable to develop critical social skills that will allow the child to learn to communicate, show empathy, or share with other people.

A parent may isolate a child out of fear for the child's safety or as a reflection of the parent's own depression. Regardless of reason, such harsh and unreasonable isolation deprives a child of the opportunity to develop socially and emotionally. When older, these children may rebel and be unable to negotiate healthy relationships. They may become an easy mark and be victimized, or they may lash out at others in ways that we read about in the news.

Another type of emotional abuse is exploiting or corrupting a child. With this type of abuse, a child is exposed to situations or behaviors that are not appropriate. For example, six-year-old Miranda's father invited her to watch pornography with him. "She needs to know about the world and what to avoid," he explained to me.

Nine-year-old Lequisha was asked by her father to dress up

for him and his buddies and then encouraged to dance seductively as she undressed in front of them. When her drunken father collapsed, so did his ability to protect his daughter.

These examples show that other types of abuse often accompany emotional abuse. By itself, emotional abuse is rarely

Emotional abuse scars the hearts and minds of our children in ways that are not easily healed.

reported and even less often substantiated. Unfortunately, it's just too hard to prove. According to most legal definitions, an offender of emotional abuse can only be prosecuted if the harm to the child can be observed or measured.

An emotionally abused child is affected in many ways. The child may direct the anger outward and become physically or verbally aggressive toward others. Or, the child may turn the pain inward and suffer low self-esteem and feelings of incompetence, and as an adolescent, become at risk for depression, drug and alcohol abuse, or suicide.

When my students and I asked churches which type of child abuse and neglect was the most important to them, they consistently responded that each type is important and that each causes damage to children. Consistently, church leaders expressed concern over emotional abuse in their church families. Respondents acknowledged that some parents yell too much at their children or call them degrading names. This was particularly true, they felt, of parents of adolescents. At the same time, church leaders did not seem to know how to respond to these situations. They wanted to maintain a positive relationship with the parents and not offend them, and yet saw the damage that emotional abuse does to children.

Our response to emotional abuse

 How can we protect children from emotional abuse? One thing we can do in our faith communities is to watch our words in all situations. Whether drinking coffee during fellowship time, disagreeing at a business meeting, or shingling a roof, we must choose to use words that are uplifting and pleasing to God. Other people, old and young alike, are listening to us and learning from our behavior.

Scripture commands us to bridle our tongues. Matthew 12:36-37 reminds us that we will be held accountable for every word we speak. Ephesians 4:31-32 calls on us to be kind and to rid ourselves of all harsh words: "Get rid of all bitterness, rage, anger, harsh words, and slander, as well as all types of evil behavior. Instead, be kind to each other, tenderhearted, forgiving one another, just as God through Christ has forgiven you."

In addition to modeling positive interactions, we can invite parents to learn about the effects of emotional abuse on their children. Through a parenting class or a home visit, parents may be able to grasp the harm their words do to their children and learn to replace these abusive behaviors with ones that are positive, nurturing, and helpful. Parents can learn about positive communication, especially with teenage children.

If you are concerned that a child is being emotionally abused, consider reporting it to the CPS or the police. While your report may not provide the evidence required for the authorities to intervene, it may accompany concerns reported by others and be enough to prompt an investigation. Even if emotional abuse is never substantiated, a report to the authorities may prompt services being offered to the family that will help long-term.

Of all types of abuse, each of us certainly has the capacity to commit acts of emotional abuse. With genuine humility let us confess our careless acts and know that God will help us to set things right. When children experience emotional abuse, we must be ready and able to recognize it and know what to do.

Discussion Questions

1. Why do you think the author says that neglect is one of the most difficult types of abuse to confront and change?
2. You become worried about a young child whom you often see playing outside unsupervised. You are especially wor-

ried that the child will fall into a nearby creek. You are aware that the child's father is not in the picture and that the child's mother is struggling to make ends meet. You want to help, but you don't want to offend the mother. What can you do?

3. What do you think is the biggest need for families and children in your community: housing, food, clothing, jobs, healthcare, childcare, education, or something else?

4. Share an example of emotional abuse that you have witnessed. How did it make you feel? What did you want to do? What did you actually do?

5. During a small group gathering in church, a father repeatedly yells at his young children in a way that seems inappropriate to you. What do you do?

Action Items

1. Go to an area that is very different socioeconomically from your own. Better yet, do your grocery shopping at a store in that neighborhood. When you observe children or families, what do you see that is positive? What do you see that concerns or surprises you?

2. Donate food, clothing, books, or toys to an organization that serves families.

3. Ask a single parent whom you know what you can do to help.

4. Read Genesis 15–22 and take note of the parents' actions. In what ways are children in the story valued and kept safe? In what ways does it seem that children are not valued nor kept safe?

5. Count how many times you hear someone criticize a church member or coworker this week. If possible, offer a kind word.

Chapter 6

A Look at Physical Abuse

"Love is patient and kind."

—*1 Corinthians 13:4a*

The physical abuse of a child is unthinkable. Perhaps we have seen the gruesome pictures of children who have been beaten and battered, even killed, by their caretakers. But until we have experienced or observed physical abuse with our own eyes, it is easy to deny that it occurs. How could someone deliberately hurt a child? Perhaps those of us who are parents can understand a little.

Remember that really rough week you had awhile back? That one where your boss gave you an unreasonable deadline, and then told you that he absolutely could not authorize any overtime for you to meet the deadline? You came home on Thursday and found your nine-year-old son had put his skateboard through the dining room window. Stomping off across the house to find your son, you find your three-year-old daughter licking marshmallows and sticking them to the oil painting you bought last week but hadn't had the chance to hang yet. Your heart is really pumping now! You pick up your daughter, who naturally puts her sticky fingers around your neck and in your hair, and you begin to yell at her.

Could you perhaps see this scene deteriorating into one where physical harm is done to a child? At this point, an abusive parent may reach for a belt or wire hanger and begin to hit the child out of sheer anger and frustration. The child would likely scream and try to escape, but the parent would catch the child and deliver not one but many more blows. If the abusive parent is experienced at this abuse, he may remember to hit the child in places that can be easily covered by clothing so the child can go to school the next day and not have to explain the bruises and welts. The non-abusive parent would be able to take some deep breaths, clean the child's hands, and begin to think constructively and creatively about ways to resolve the problems that respect the children's developmental levels and personalities.

Five types of physical abuse:

- Bruises, welts, and lacerations
- Broken bones
- Burns
- Shaken baby syndrome

The minimum standards set by federal legislation in the U.S. for physical abuse are: "Physical injury (ranging from minor bruises to severe fractures or death) as a result of punching, beating, kicking, biting, shaking, throwing, stabbing, choking, hitting (with a hand, stick, strap, or other object), burning, or otherwise harming a child. Such injury is considered abuse regardless of whether the caretaker intended to hurt the child."[1] (The definitions used in Canadian provinces and territories are similar.)

Physical abuse may have occurred if a child's injury is unexplained, not consistent with the explanation given, or is non-accidental. Knowledge of child development is important when considering whether or not a child's injury is accidental. When you are told by a four-year-old girl that she skinned her knee by falling on the sidewalk, you can probably believe the story to be true. Especially when she also shows you her skinned elbow. However, if a two-month-old baby shows up in the emergency room with a broken arm and the mother says that the baby caught his arm in the rails of the crib while rolling over, you will want to ask more questions.

Bruises, welts, and lacerations

About two-thirds of children who are investigated by the authorities for possible physical abuse have received bruises and welts on their back, buttocks, face, neck, abdomen, or back of their legs. These are not places where you would expect a bruise if a child fell or ran into something. These are marks left when a child is deliberately struck with a belt, extension cord, hairbrush, clothes hanger, or any other object that was within reach. Sometimes the mark was left by the human hand. Often, the imprint of the object can be seen on the child's skin. Any bruise or laceration to a child's face is of significant concern.

Broken bones

Physical abuse may also be seen in the form of broken bones. Dr. Henry Kempe first coined the term *battered child syndrome* in 1962 when looking for an explanation for skeletal injuries. A very young child may receive broken ribs from being shaken or a skull fracture from being thrown down on a counter. A collar bone may be broken when a frustrated parent jerks a child around by the arm.

When a child receives an accidental injury, the parent is likely to seek medical treatment promptly. A child with a non-accidental skeletal injury may not be taken for treatment until days later when it becomes apparent that the injury will not just go away. When x-rayed, such a child may show many other fractures in various stages of healing. This is when questions need to be answered regarding the source of the child's injuries.

Burns

Another type of physical abuse is burns. These burns may come from a cigarette or hot water. I worked with a family that consisted of a mother, boyfriend, and three-year-old Camilia. The child had been taken to the emergency room with severe sock burns to her feet and calves. The mother said that she had left her child in the care of her boyfriend while she went to work. When she returned home and inquired about the burns to her daughter's feet, her boyfriend said that Camilia had climbed into the bathtub before he had had a chance to check the water temperature. When the doctors saw the severity of the burns coupled with the straight burn line around each of her leg calves, the authorities were called.

By checking the water heater in the apartment, they determined that the water could not have come out of the tap hot enough to have caused the severity of the burns. In addition, a child who voluntarily climbs into a bathtub filled with hot water would not have a straight burn line. She would show either a couple of toes burned, or splash burns on her legs and perhaps other parts of her body as she attempted to get out of the water.

It was determined that the boyfriend had heated water on the stove and poured it into the kitchen sink. He forcibly held the girl's feet in the water. The reason he gave for his behavior was that Camilia had defecated in her underwear, and he wanted to teach her a lesson by cleaning her in this way. Although Camilia has endured at least six surgeries to repair the skin damage, she will bear scars of this horrific physical abuse for the rest of her life.

Shaken baby syndrome

One type of physical abuse that has hit the headlines recently is shaken baby syndrome. As we all know, babies cry. Sometimes they cry a lot. When you mix a crying baby with a tired or frustrated parent or an adult who is unfamiliar with the care of the child, the child is at risk for being shaken.

Shaken baby syndrome occurs when the caretaker, often male, picks up and shakes a baby to silence the cries. This is not a light or playful jiggle, but a violent thrusting, which causes the baby's head to be thrown back and forth. The baby's immature brain sloshes around in the skull and receives serious bruising. The brain swells. The retina of the baby's eye may hemorrhage or become detached. The baby often suffers bruises and skeletal injuries as a result of the harsh handling.

The offender's behavior may be reinforced as the child typically does stop crying as a result of the shaking. The child may fall asleep and wake later with vomiting, lethargy, or irritability. Or, the child may slip into a coma or die. If the baby does survive the shaking, she may be blind or paralyzed, suffer from seizures, be profoundly retarded, or have learning disabilities.

Fetal Alcohol Spectrum Disorder (FASD) and Alcohol-Related Neurodevelopmental Disorder (ARND)

Before babies are born, they can be significantly hurt by their mothers' drinking of alcohol. Children with Fetal Alcohol Spectrum Disorder (FASD) or Alcohol-Related Neurodevelopmental Disorder (ARND) suffer irreversible brain damage and have a broad range of physical defects and levels of severity in mental functioning. FASD is the leading cause of mental retardation in the United States. While perhaps not categorized as abuse or neglect, the mother may unknowingly damage the fetus by drinking before she even knows she is pregnant. Sadly, the greatest damage to a fetus occurs in the first trimester when the most basic functions are being formed. Other substances, including cigarettes, methamphetamine, cocaine, marijuana, and heroin also cause injury to an unborn baby.

Our response to physical abuse

Each type of physical abuse is completely preventable. Notice I did not say "easily" preventable. If you see an easy solution to any of these types of abuse, then you do not fully understand the problem.

The complexities of these situations are overwhelming and unique to each family. While one parent may benefit from a group parenting class, another may need employment and childcare. While one family may be strengthened significantly through a weekly home visit by a social worker, another may need residential treatment for a drug addiction. Most families could benefit from increased social support, meaning somewhere to turn when they need help or just want to talk or have fun.

Physical abuse is completely preventable.

Can the faith community play a role in preventing physical abuse? Absolutely! The church has resources—spiritual, emotional, physical—that can have a significant positive impact on struggling families. Children need to know that the church in their neighborhood cares about them, that their neighbor enjoys playing basketball with them and that their teacher wants to help them be safe. Parents need to know that the church in their neighborhood is ready and able to help them.

Are we ready for children and families to look to us for help? What do we have to offer? When do we need to turn to other organizations for help? Remember: If you see any mark on a child that is unexplained, please report this to CPS or the police as soon as possible.

Physical punishment

Physical punishment is difficult for our faith communities to grapple with. Some scriptures seem to give us contradictory messages on the use of physical punishment. "Spare the rod and spoil the child" is often cited as justification for inflicting physical harm on a child. In fact, several verses in the Old

Testament book of Proverbs refer to this *rod* as a necessary component for childrearing.

In probably the most cited passage, the Bible reads, "Those who spare the rod of discipline hate their children. Those who love their children care enough to discipline them" (Proverbs 13:24). Proverbs 22:15 states, "A youngster's heart is filled with foolishness, but physical discipline will drive it far away." Proverbs 23:13-14 advocates for this *rod* even more, mandating, "Don't fail to discipline your children. They won't die if you spank them. Physical discipline may well save them from death."

In the book of Psalms, however, this same *rod* is said to have given King David comfort (23:4). The rod spoken of in both Proverbs and Psalms is actually the rod used by shepherds to care for their sheep in biblical times. The Hebrew word for this is *shebet*, used specifically for the following purposes: (1) to throw in front of wandering sheep to bring them back to the flock, (2) to scare off an intruding animal and protect the sheep, (3) to count the sheep, (4) to part the sheep's wool to examine the skin for disease, and (5) to symbolize the guardianship of a shepherd over the sheep.

No evidence exists to suggest that the rod is used physically to harm or punish sheep. In fact, scholars have noted that the Hebrew word for discipline, *yasar*, is not necessarily a negative punitive discipline, but rather implies an equally balanced term. Along with meaning "to chasten, correct, punish," it also carries with it an equal meaning of "admonish, exhort, instruct," implying that all discipline must carry love and appropriateness, as a shepherd would to his sheep—his livelihood.[2]

Spanking is often touted as a God-given right of parents. Well-meaning parents and grandparents have proclaimed to me that if parents would just spank their children more often, we wouldn't have such big problems with juvenile delinquency and crime. Again, these are simple solutions to complex problems.

Rather than punish our children for wrongdoing, I suggest that we discipline them. The difference is basic. To *punish* is "to subject to pain, loss, confinement or death, etc., as a penalty for some offense, transgression, or fault."[3] Whereas *discipline* is an "activity, exercise, or regimen that develops or improves a skill; training."[4] The purpose of discipline is to teach, to provide guidance, to help children develop self-discipline. Discipline should teach respect, bring knowledge, and build self-worth.

Spanking teaches a child it is okay for a bigger person to hit a smaller person or to be more sneaky next time and not get caught. Spanking also runs the risk of further angering the child and causing the child to lose heart (see Ephesians 6:4 and Colossians 3:21). Someone who spanks a child also runs the risk of becoming overwhelmed with anger and seriously hurting the child. As a follower of Jesus, I cannot picture Jesus spanking a child. Rather, I picture Jesus welcoming and respecting children while also calling them to right action.

> The purpose of discipline is to teach, to provide guidance, to help children develop self-discipline.

Consider the many other tools you have available to you in your discipline toolbox: noticing and encouraging good behavior, using praise and rewards, listening actively, or allowing natural consequences. You can also give choices, clearly communicate your expectations, or seek a deeper understanding of your child's developmental level and personality. If the child is young, you can use distraction or simply remove your child from a dangerous situation. Learn more by exploring any of the parenting curricula in appendix 1.

As followers of Jesus, let us seek nonviolent ways to solve conflicts and to discipline our children. Our children are placed in our care for a few years as gifts from heaven. We will answer to God for the ways that we handle these precious gifts.

Discussion Questions

1. Consider the example of the stressed-out parent in the beginning of this chapter. What do you suggest this parent do?
2. Share an experience of physical discipline. From both the

perspective of the parent and the child, how do you feel the physical discipline did or did not work?

3. What is the difference between physical discipline and physical abuse? Consider the characteristics and results of each in your response.
4. What could your church do to prevent shaken baby syndrome?
5. The author states that child abuse is "completely preventable" but not "easily preventable." Do you agree or disagree? Why?
6. In what ways might the preaching or teaching of your church unwittingly encourage physical abuse?
7. What can the church do to prevent physical abuse?

Action Items

1. Come up with a list of ten creative ways to discipline a child. Discuss these with a friend.
2. Offer to babysit for someone this week.
3. Read more about shaken baby syndrome on the Internet or at your library.
4. Reflect in a journal about how you were disciplined as a child and how this was helpful or not helpful. What did it teach you? Did it help you learn right behavior? How did it affect your relationship with your parent(s)?

Chapter 7

A Look at Sexual Abuse

I can never escape from your Spirit! I can never get away from your presence! . . . How precious are your thoughts about me, O God. They cannot be numbered!

—Psalm 139:7, 17

Tracy is fifteen years old and an active member of her church's youth group. Funny, witty, and eager for attention, Tracy is emerging as a leader in her youth group. Pastor Eric is new to the congregation. He is married and has two preschool children. Tracy's family has experienced numerous tragedies, including the loss of Tracy's father and older brother in a car accident eight years ago. Tracy's mother works two jobs, trying to make ends meet for Tracy and her two younger brothers. Not only is Tracy hungry for a father-figure, but she is often left unsupervised. When she was twelve, Tracy was groped at a school-sponsored haunted house. Embarrassed, she didn't tell anyone.

Pastor Eric begins to hold private Bible studies with Tracy in his church office. After a couple of weeks, Pastor Eric invites Tracy to a Christian music concert in a nearby town with the plan to stop at an area park to complete their "Bible study." Eager for attention from a male spiritual mentor, Tracy accepts Pastor Eric's invitation. Pastor Eric continues to find occasion to be alone with Tracy, and at his suggestion, Tracy tells her mother that she is out with some members of the youth group.

Within months, the stops in the park for Bible study begin to occur after dark, and Pastor Eric starts to verbally express his admiration for Tracy. He confides in Tracy that his wife is often too busy with caring for the children and not able to attend to his needs. He is overwhelmed by the needs of the congregation and says he always feels so energized after spending time with Tracy. Pastor Eric's emotional overtures soon become physical as he reaches out to touch Tracy's hand or to brush back her hair. He gives her gifts of jewelry. He tells Tracy that they have a special relationship and that if she tells anyone, others might be jealous and that would ruin everything.

Tracy feels confused by her feelings. She really enjoys the time spent with Pastor Eric. She likes the feeling of being special in the eyes of someone as important as a minister of her church. The gifts are awfully nice, much too expensive for her mother to be able to afford. Yet, Tracy wonders if the things she and Pastor Eric are beginning to do together are appropriate.

She'd like to talk with her mom about the ways Pastor Eric is beginning to touch her but is afraid her mother will overreact or not believe her. Maybe it is better to stay quiet a little longer. But then Pastor Eric becomes bolder in his actions toward Tracy, moving to kissing her hand, then her cheek. When he invites Tracy to go camping with him, Tracy writes him a note explaining her feelings and telling him that she cannot spend any more time with him. She puts the note in Pastor Eric's mailbox at church.

The note falls out of the pastor's mailbox and is found and read by the church secretary. The secretary takes the note to the lead pastor. In disbelief, the lead pastor immediately confronts Pastor Eric, who outright denies any inappropriate relationship with Tracy. Pastor Eric tells the lead pastor and later the deacons that Tracy is lonely and has been angry with him for canceling a youth field trip—this must be her way of seeking revenge. Wanting to avoid a widespread problem and acknowledging the effective ministry of Pastor Eric with the youth, the church leaders side with Pastor Eric. Hoping to avoid future problems, they ask Pastor Eric to report monthly to the lead pastor about his activities with the youth group.

Meanwhile, no one speaks to Tracy. Tracy becomes confused and saddened by the sudden loss of attention from Pastor Eric. She refuses to go to church and to participate in any youth activities. She skips school, and her grades drop. Having become accustomed to lying to her mother about time spent with Pastor Eric, she now lies about the alcohol that she drinks at parties with her new friends. Once, she tries to tell her mother about what happened with Pastor Eric, but her mother gets mad and tells her that she is "sick and tired of Tracy's lies." Tracy's behaviors spiral downward.

In this situation, Tracy was not protected by the adults around her. She was repeatedly placed in a vulnerable spot, which allowed an offender to prey on her. Her simple trust in an authority figure, a spiritual mentor and one many years her elder, blinded her to the progression of his inappropriate advances. She enjoyed the attention, the gifts. And yet she was taken advantage of. She was hurt. Her trust was betrayed. Her future relationships with others, both male and female, will forever be changed. Her relationship with God and the church will take time, counseling, and prayer to be fully restored, if it ever can be.

Pastor Eric needs to be held accountable for his behaviors. His professional sexual misconduct must be addressed. This serious violation of a sacred trust must be reported both to local authorities and to denominational leaders. Bold steps must be taken to ensure that there are no more victims.

Sexual abuse

Nothing is as insidious as the sexual abuse of children. Given a choice, we would prefer to deny that child sexual abuse happens. Of any type of abuse or neglect, this is the type that is most likely to haunt our churches. While our faith communities certainly have a role in preventing neglect and physical abuse, this abuse occurs most often within families and living situations. But sexual abuse can also occur within organizations like churches.

If we are to protect our children, we must once and for all shake the notion that sexual abuse occurs at the hands of strangers who jump out from behind bushes and attack our children with brutal force. Sadly, that does happen, but not nearly as often as it does at the hands of parents, stepparents, grandparents, siblings, teachers, coaches, and youth ministers—family and friends whom the child knows and loves. Physical force is rarely necessary as the offender entices and deceives the child.

In the United States, sexual abuse is defined as:

> the employment, use, persuasion, inducement, enticement, or coercion of any child to engage in, or assist any other person to engage in, any sexually explicit conduct or simulation of such conduct for the purpose of producing a visual depiction of such conduct; or the rape, and in cases of caretaker or inter-familial relationships, statutory rape, molestation, prostitution, or other form of sexual exploitation of children, or incest with children.[1]

Sexual abuse can also be defined as "any act occurring between people who are at different developmental stages which is for the sexual gratification of the person at the more advanced developmental stage."[2] It may include oral, anal, or genital penetration, or other forms of genital contact or touching of intimate body parts.

Unlike other types of abuse that victimize boys and girls equally, the sexual abuse victim is more often female. In Canada girls were four times more likely than boys to be sexually assaulted by a family member, particularly girls between twelve and fifteen.[3] In the United States girls were five times more likely to be sexually abused than boys.[4] Boys are by no means immune from sexual abuse. Sadly, boys also experience sexual abuse and may encounter additional barriers to reporting. Boys are typically socialized to be strong and independent, not needing to ask for help or protection. When a sexual offender preys on a male child, the child's response may be heightened by gender issues and expectations. If the abuse is male-on-male, the child may have added confusion around sexual identity. Additionally, we may not be as protective or suspicious of inappropriate relationships with boys as we are with girls.

The offender of sexual abuse is most often male. In Canada in 2007, 96 percent of sexual assaults by a family member were committed by a male, with 36 percent by a male extended family member, 32 percent by a father, and 27 percent by a brother.[5] Offenders may also be female or females working together with males. Although a female may sometimes overtly cooperate with a male partner, her participation is usually more subtle, but no less damaging. Sometimes a mother may have some level of knowledge of the sexual abuse but does not act to protect the child for fear of losing her partner or his income.

We must understand that an offender does not just sexually abuse a child one day without warning; rather, there is usually a long, methodical period of grooming before the sexual abuse ever comes to fruition. As with the story about Tracy, a youth leader, uncle, or stepbrother may spend weeks, months, even years developing a relationship with and gaining access to a child before ever beginning to touch the child inappropriately. The offender will likely shower the child with gifts, work on convincing her that she is special, and plant the seeds of isolation and secrecy before he begins sexually abusive acts.

By the time he reaches the point of sexual contact, the child is brainwashed into believing that she is special in the eyes of the offender, that she alone is able to meet his needs, and that if she tells anyone about the things they do together, she or her family or her pet will be hurt. Often, the child is confused by the sexual abuse. She may be ashamed of the things she does with her father, perhaps even blaming herself for them.

Hearing all this, you can perhaps understand why sexual

abuse often occurs many times over a long period of time. The child victim often does not tell anyone about the abuse for a long time, and may even deny outright that the abuse is occurring. An offender often has multiple victims before being caught, if he is ever caught. Sexual abuse often goes unreported or is not reported until years later.

When a child does tell someone about the sexual abuse, the immediate response is extremely critical. Unfortunately, as was the case with Tracy, the child-victim is not always heard or believed. This is tragic for the child in a multitude of ways: the abuse is allowed to continue, the child may not ever speak of the abuse again, and the child is denied the help he or she desperately needs to overcome the abuse experienced.

As churches, parents, and caretakers, we must be sensitive to what children are trying to tell us and respond with calmness and compassion. A child's outcry will be couched in a child's vocabulary and style, which may mean it is revealed in behavior, a drawing, a letter, or spoken words. Depending on the child's age, the child will not likely walk up to you and say, "Pastor Tom is sexually abusing me." Rather, the child may tell you, "Cousin Joe puts his pee-pee in my pee-pee." The child may also show you with his actions, such as by becoming withdrawn from normal activities. When asked if something is wrong, the child may begin to cry and not be able to put it easily into words. Or, the child may become abnormally aggressive, perhaps approaching peers in a sexual manner.

The effects of child sexual abuse on the child

The effects of child sexual abuse are devastating and varied. Many children become depressed and withdraw from normal activities; others become aggressive and display seductive behaviors. School-age children's grades may drop as they are unable to concentrate on academic work. They may engage in inappropriate sexualized play and demonstrate a premature understanding of sex. As youth, the abuse victim may turn to alcohol or drugs to drown out the memories, may encourage sexual relationships with peers, and perhaps become pregnant at an early age. As one young mother who had been sexually abused told me, "The only thing I can do well is have cute babies." Her whole identity was wrapped up in her ability to have sex with multiple partners and produce beautiful babies. Her self-worth had been stripped from her by this behavior to the point that she had come to believe her only role in society was to have sex and produce babies.

Many survivors of sexual abuse experience post-traumatic stress disorder or related symptoms, such as recurring memories in the form of flashbacks, nightmares, and intrusive thoughts. Many abuse victims deal with the sexual abuse episodes by dissociating—by denying the physical sensations of what is occurring and focusing on something else in the room or in their mind. Later, as a survivor, they may continue this pattern of dis-association by turning to drugs and alcohol.

Many survivors have difficulty developing positive relationships with friends, particularly in the area of trust. They have been hurt by someone closest to them and are reluctant to trust again, to open themselves up to that kind of pain.

The survivor will likely seek to avoid whatever context the abuse occurred in. For example, if the abuse occurred at church or at the hands of a church member, the survivor will be reluctant to return to that church or any church. Additionally, if the survivor later becomes a parent, the survivor will be very reluctant to allow his or her own child to engage in church activities.

Our response to sexual abuse

 Too often the church tries to handle sexual abuse by itself. Perhaps the church does not truly believe the abuse occurred. Perhaps the church wants to avoid negative publicity. Well-intentioned, many churches think they can take care of it themselves, and, sadly, this often denies the child the help she

needs and gives the offender further opportunity to sexually abuse the same child or others.

Unless we are professionals in the field of child abuse, we should not probe the child for details. Children are easily led by our questions and will react to our emo-

As churches, parents, and care-takers, we must be sensitive to what children are trying to tell us.

tions. Additionally, when we ask a child to tell his or her story over and over to different people, we are not only contaminating the story but also re-victimizing the child.

The church is not equipped to handle the complex nature of sexual abuse but rather must join in partnership with local professionals who can assist in keeping the child safe, gathering evidence, and bringing hope and restoration to the child and non-offending family members. As soon as possible, we must report suspected sexual abuse to the authorities. Many communities now have child advocacy centers where forensic interviewers are trained in talking with children, in getting the information needed to protect the child and to proceed with a prosecution, and to put services in place for the child and family.

The church is most certainly not helpless to prevent sexual abuse. Many policies and actions can be taken to protect our children. A first important step is to make sure a child is never alone with an adult. The two-adult rule is an important one, made stronger when the two adults are unrelated to one another. Plan ahead so a child is not alone with an adult in a vehicle, especially a female child with a male adult. Windows in all classrooms and doors are important and send the message that all activities in the church can be observed by others. Background checks on all church staff and volunteers not only help to screen out potential sexual abuse offenders, but they also alert everyone to the reality of abuse. (These steps are outlined in a later chapter.)

By enacting protective measures, we protect not only our children, but also ourselves. Preventive measures may protect us from false allegations. For example, if a conversation with a child is overheard and a misunderstanding happens, having had a second adult present may be all it takes to have protected yourself. All allegations of abuse need serious attention. If the allegations are reported and deemed false, professional attention is still necessary to determine if the allegations were a cry for help.

Sexual offenders are in your community, and they are looking.

Look around your church. How easy might it be for a sexual offender to be alone with one of your children? Take a serious look at your church's programs. How easy might it be for a sexual offender to develop a close relationship with a child or teen? If a sexual offender were looking for a way to get access to children, how likely is the offender to pick your church? Do you look like an easy target? Take your safety procedures seriously, and make them public. You will likely never know the good they are doing in protecting your children.

Discussion Questions

1. What role did Tracy play in being sexually abused? What role did each of these adults play in Tracy being sexually abused: Pastor Eric, Tracy's mother, the secretary, the lead pastor, the deacons, Tracy's friends, Pastor Eric's wife? Who was responsible for the sexual abuse?
2. What do you think should be done about Pastor Eric?
3. Should Tracy be asked to forgive Pastor Eric?
4. If you were the lead pastor or deacon, what would be the step-by-step procedures you could have taken in this situation? How might the outcome have been different?
5. What could the church have done to prevent Tracy from being sexually abused?
6. In what ways are the children in your church vulnerable to a sexual abuse offender? In what ways are the children in your church protected from a sexual abuse offender?

7. What do we need to do protect our children from sexual abuse?

Action Items

1. Walk around your church and look for places where someone could be alone with a child. Look for rooms without windows in the door and rooms with locks on the doors. If you find any problematic areas, talk with whoever is responsible for your church facilities about making these places safer for children.
2. Locate and read your church's policy on child safety and protection.
3. Consider the programs and services offered through your church. In what situations may the two-adult rule be compromised?
4. Speak with the children's education director about what information children and youth in your church get about healthy sexuality, sexual abuse, rape, and dating violence.

Chapter 8

Risk and Protective Factors

Let all who take refuge in you rejoice; let them sing joyful praises for-ever. Spread your protection over them, that all who love your name may be filled with joy.

—*Psalm 5:11*

We seem to be hardwired to want to know why things happen. "What caused Sue Ann to burn her son?" "Why would a Sunday school teacher molest a student?" These questions are certainly compelling and important. After all, if we want to end child abuse, don't we need to first figure out what starts or causes child abuse? Researchers have worked hard on this question for decades, and they have not come up with a simple or straightforward answer. I don't expect they ever will.

Researchers have identified risk factors that place a child or family at higher risk for child abuse. We still cannot say that any one risk factor or constellation of risk factors causes child abuse, but we can say that the greater number of risk factors, the higher likelihood that a child will be hurt.

The most significant risk factors identified for child abuse are parental history of abuse, poverty, domestic violence, parental substance abuse, parental stress, mental health, and children with disabilities. None of these factors singularly causes child abuse, but the presence of any of these factors puts a child at greater risk. The higher number of risk factors present, the more a child is at risk for abuse.

Fortunately, researchers are also working to identify protective factors. These are the factors that help to protect a child from being abused. Like risk factors, these factors may be characteristics of the family or the child. And again, no single protective factor can ensure that a child will not be abused, but the more protective factors present, the safer the child. While risk factors increase a child's vulnerability to abuse and neglect, protective factors provide buffers; they moderate and protect against these vulnerabilities.

Some children are amazingly resilient. They have the ability to rise above adversity and not appear to be negatively affected by serious trouble and hardship. Individual characteristics of a child may help to protect that child from long-term harm. These protective characteristics include optimism, self-esteem, intelligence, creativity, humor, and independence.[1]

Nevertheless, as adults, we must do all we can to keep children safe and not expose them to more stressors than they should have to handle. Family protective factors are generally considered to be parenting knowledge and skills along with social support. I would like to add faith and church participation as a protective factor. Risk and protective factors are discussed in this chapter.

Risk Factors:	Protective Factors:
• Poverty	• Parenting knowledge and skills
• Domestic violence	• Social support
• Substance abuse	• Faith and church participation
• Parental stress	

Risk factor: poverty

Research shows a very strong correlation between poverty and child abuse and neglect. One study showed that the poorest children were three times more likely to suffer child abuse than children in families with incomes between $15,000 and $29,000, and twenty-five times more likely than were children in the most affluent categories.[2] However, it is important to realize that most poor families do not abuse or neglect their children.

Child abuse happens in families at all income levels and in churches in all types of communities. It is probable that child abuse in lower-income families and communities is more visible. Child abuse in more affluent families can be more easily hidden as these families have access to more resources and are under less scrutiny by social services. Nevertheless, kids in poor families are at greater risk due to the availability of fewer services, ongoing stress of living in poor conditions, lack of safety, and less parenting education.

Our faith communities have a lot to offer families in poverty. We are called to bring good news to the poor (Matthew 11:5, Luke 4:18, Luke 7:22). Consider the example of the early Christians in Acts 2:45, "They sold their property and possessions and shared the money with those in need." And answer the question in 1 John 3:17: "If someone has enough money to live well and sees a brother or sister in need but shows no compassion—how can God's love be in that person?"

Our provision of food, shelter, and clothing can make a significant and positive impact on a poor family. When parents do not need to be so worried about meeting daily needs, they can spend more physical and emotional resources on meeting the less tangible but other important needs of their children—like helping with homework, giving a hug, and reading a story.

Risk factor: domestic violence

Violence between parents or directed at a parent is a huge risk factor for children. In Canada child welfare workers reported in 2003 that 51 percent of female caregivers in their investigations were negatively affected by domestic violence.[3] In the United States, 24 percent of child abuse victims had a caregiver at risk for domestic violence.[4] Many times, the abuse is directed at the children as well as the female caregiver, but even if it is not, the children hear and feel it in the home. Statistics Canada reports, "Almost 40 percent of women assaulted by spouses said their children witnessed the violence against them (either directly or indirectly) and in many cases the violence was severe. In half of cases of spousal violence against women that were witnessed by children, the woman feared for her life."[5]

A battered woman is often reluctant to report suspected child abuse for fear of losing custody of her children. Child protective and legal systems in both United States and Canada struggle to respond to situations where domestic violence and child abuse overlap.

Domestic violence frightens children, as it does all of us. Children live with fear for their own well-being as well as for the well-being of their mother. Children, especially sons, often seek to protect their mother—sometimes by jumping on the back of the man to try and stop the beating, as was the case in a family I knew.

Children in families with domestic violence often also take on too much responsibility. Feeling the violence is somehow their fault, they cover for their family, help with cleaning up the aftermath, and become confidants for their mother as they consider ways to be safe.

A faith community must be very, very careful when seeking to help a family with domestic violence issues. The faith community can play a part in strengthening families and protecting children, but once domestic violence is present, the dynamics are explosive. Not only must we think of our own safety when interacting with this family, but we must consider that our efforts to help may actually make things worse. Our well-intentioned visits may further anger the batterer as he seeks to isolate his family so he may continue his violent acts. Most women who are hurt or killed by a batterer received their injuries while trying to leave the situation.

When domestic violence is present, the faith community must partner with local authorities and professionals to intervene effectively. The faith community can also learn more about the cycle of violence and about the effects of violence on women and children. Call a local domestic violence shelter today and see what you can do to help.

Risk factor: substance abuse

Another difficult but real risk factor for children and families is substance abuse. Whether it is alcohol, marijuana, cocaine, or methamphetamine, substance abuse hurts children and families. In Canada in 2003, child welfare workers reported that nearly one-third (30 percent) of male caregivers in their investigations abused alcohol.[6] Physical abuse may occur when parents are high or drunk and not fully aware of the consequences of their actions. Sexual abuse may occur when parents are under the influence or unable to protect their children. Neglect certainly occurs as families' resources are spent on obtaining the substance rather than paying bills and buying food and when parents are high or drunk every day and unable to meet the needs of their children.

Substance abuse not only hurts kids, but it can also cause children to stay in foster care for an extended period of time as parents struggle with their addictions. Addictions to activities such as gambling have many of the same effects as addictions to substances.

Similar to domestic violence, the church must be very careful when working with families with substance abuse issues. People who are dependent on a substance, whatever it is, are

 often very manipulative. I have seen how an individual with an addiction can hold a whole church emotionally hostage as he asks for help but continues to feed his addiction. The church wants so badly to provide the help but is not prepared to see through the addictive behavior to realize that they are actually perpetuating the substance abuse. Professional help is needed to treat substance abuse. The faith community can be there to support the family, to stand with them through treatment, and most importantly, to provide a safe house for the children.

Risk factor: parental stress

We all act and react differently when we are under stress, right? On a calm day, I could tolerate my six-year-old's whining all right, but on a day when I was stressed out, I was not so tolerant. The amount of stress that many at risk families are under is phenomenal. If I were a single mother with three preschoolers, a minimum-wage job, no reliable transportation, and a broken water pipe in my kitchen, then I would really know stress.

Under stress, we respond in a fight-or-flight fashion, which is not good for parenting, especially on a daily basis. Many families live in a chronic state of crisis, partly because of poverty, partly because of poor decision-making, partly because of bad luck. A stressed-out parent is more likely to physically or sexually abuse children or to be unable to recognize and appropriately respond to a child's needs.

We find examples in the Bible of mothers under insurmountable stress while struggling to care for their children. Think of the anguish of Hagar when Abraham banished her and her young son to the desert. When their small ration of food and water was gone, Hagar laid her son under a bush and stepped away from him—still near enough to protect him from predators but not so near as to have to hear him cry or watch him die. As the story unfolds in Genesis 21, God hears the child's cries and provides water for his mother to give him. And God remains with this small, single-parent family and helps them survive in the desert.

In 1 Kings 17 we encounter the plight of a widow and her son who have reached the very end of their food. Picture this mother as she goes out to gather sticks so she can prepare their very last loaf of bread. She has been pinching and stretching to make their flour and oil last, but now this is really it. After this loaf their food will be gone. What will she do? How can she feed her son? While caught up in her thoughts, a man calls out and asks her to give him food and drink. With a sigh, she replies, "I swear by the Lord your God that I don't have a single piece of bread in the house. And I have only a handful of flour left in the jar and a little cooking oil in the bottom of the jug. I was just gathering a few sticks to cook this last meal, and then my son and I will die" (1 Kings 17:12).

As in the previous story from Genesis, God supplies the needs of this mother and her son. The man asking for food and drink is the prophet Elijah, and he promises that if she provides him with nourishment, she and her son will have enough flour and oil to get them through this difficult time. With trust and hope, the widow complies, and in so doing, she and her son get their needs met.

 Through relationships, we too can do a lot to alleviate the stress of an at risk family. We can offer respite care to a harried parent, offer a ride to the grocery store, or go on a picnic with a family—letting the kids play and run off energy, and giving the parent a chance to talk and get some fresh air.

Providing concrete resources like employment, childcare, housing, education, and healthcare makes a huge difference in reducing the stress of low-income families and allowing them to be healthier families.

Risk factor: parental mental health

Similar to substance abuse, parents who have untreated mental health issues are not able to be fully available to their children, nor responsive to their children's needs. Maternal depression, in particular, is often linked with child neglect. I have seen a mother who was so depressed that she was not able to get off the couch or out of the apartment to adequately supervise her children, provide healthful meals, or access needed medical care. Such depression may stem from child sexual abuse, from a recent pregnancy

 (postpartum depression), or other reasons. No matter the source of the depression, the child is being hurt and/or neglected.

We can help with this risk factor by providing referrals to mental health professionals and lowering the barriers to receiving help.

Risk factor: children with disabilities

Those of us who are parents know that parenting is a challenge in the best of times. But when a child has a disability or chronic illness, the job of parent increases exponentially. Parents of children with a disability often experience high demands in their care giving, increased financial stress, and social isolation.

The disability may make the child more difficult to care for. Communication with the child may be difficult, the child may display behavioral and emotional difficulties, or the child may have a challenging temperament. The caretaker may need to be hyper-vigilant in order to keep the child safe and meet basic needs. Because of the added challenge in caring for a child with a disability, the parent may have an especially high need for respite care coupled with a particularly difficult time finding appropriate and affordable childcare.

The stress in these families can run very high, which compounds this risk factor. Far too often, I have seen the parents of a child with cerebral palsy, for example, be reported because the school finds cockroaches in the wheelchair, or a diaper that hasn't been changed since the previous school day.

Sadly, children with disabilities are much more likely to be abused or neglected. This is true for all types of abuse and neglect. An offender may prey on a disabled child because the child cannot report the abuse. A disabled child who is used to being handled, such as to be diapered or moved into a wheelchair, may have a hard time distinguishing between appropriate and inappropriate touch. The child with a disability is especially vulnerable and needs extra care and protection.

 As faith communities, we must remember to ask families with a child that is disabled how we can be of help. We must not assume that they need or want help, and we certainly must make our faith communities accessible and welcoming to them.

Protective factor: parenting knowledge and skills

When we think of parents who abuse or neglect their children, the first thing we feel is probably anger. Then we think of the child and probably get sad. Then we wish a judge would send the parents to a parenting class. Many judges and other authorities do send parents to parenting classes, and that is an important step in helping families and protecting children. Many wonderful curricula are available for such classes (see appendix 1).

As we know, good parenting does not just come instinctively. The lucky ones among us have had good parenting models—models that have shaped our responses and reactions. Others of us were not so lucky. Our parents were either not present or were doing the best they could under difficult circumstances.

Parenting classes can be very helpful in teaching child development and parenting skills and can influence parenting attitudes. Some parents, especially those who are young, need basic information on the ages and stages of children. In other words, at what age can a child be expected to be toilet trained? At what age can a child be expected to be more defiant (or, put more positively, expected to assert themselves strongly)?

These kinds of child development details are critical for all parents in forming expectations for our children. Many abusive or neglectful parents do not know these norms, and may expect too much or too little of a child.

I once knew a mother whose fourteen-month-old son was not showing any signs of walking or talking and weighed only seventeen pounds. Part of the problem was that this young mother did not have adequate knowledge of child development; she did not realize her son was grossly underweight, falling behind in his physical development, and needing help.

While risk factors increase a child's vulnerability to abuse and neglect, protective factors provide buffers; they moderate and protect against these vulnerabilities.

Another mother was aware that her nine-year-old son was defecating in his pants in school, but she did not do anything about it. Perhaps she did not realize this was really a problem. Or, like the previous mother, she was too overwhelmed with other things to realize that her son needed help. Changes in toileting behaviors can sometimes be caused by medical issues, but often they are indicators of sexual abuse, as was the case for this child.

Parenting classes are one way of providing education to parents on child development. Many classes also teach important skills like communication and discipline. Some parenting classes help parents become more self-aware and explore how this effects their parenting.

However, sending parents to a parenting class is only one component in an array of services that are needed to help families and protect children. The needs of most abusive families run much deeper and are much more complex than any parenting class alone can adequately address.

 As faith communities, we can offer parenting classes to our own members and, as a form of outreach, to people who live in our communities. We can also volunteer to be teachers, assistants, or childcare workers in community organizations that offer parenting classes. Another very effective way of communicating and modeling parenting skills is through home visitation. Call your local community organizations to inquire about volunteer opportunities.

Protective factor: social support

Have you ever felt alone? Completely alone? Could you say, "I have absolutely no one in the world to turn"? Not too many of us have felt that alone. Oh sure, we've been lonely. But usually our pride keeps us from calling a family member or a friend, not the fact that we don't have a family member or friend to call.

Many abusive or at risk parents have no social support. Child welfare workers in Canada noted that 40 percent of parents investigated for abuse or neglect lacked social support.[7] Perhaps they are estranged from their family because of abuse they experienced at the hands of family members. So, yes, they have family, but they aren't on good terms with them. Other times, their family is in worse shape than they are. So it simply isn't possible to turn to family members for help or support because help and support are not available. Sometimes when a parent is doing better—has a job or is learning and using new parenting skills, for example—her family members become jealous, make accusations, or make demands that drain her. Bottom line: family support is not always a possibility.

So, how about social support in the form of friends? There again, depending on where you live, good and healthy friends may not be available. Additionally, many at risk parents do not have the social skills needed to develop and maintain healthy friendships. Many of the mothers I have worked with distrusted the people in their neighborhood—saying they were all lazy, no-good gossips who were using drugs. On the list of important things to do, keeping a roof over their heads and food on their table rose above forming positive and healthy relationships.

Other elements of a community social support network include church, childcare, medical care, housing, and police protection. Especially for a family on the edge economically, the availability of these types of services is critical. Regardless of whether these services are utilized, parents need to know the services are there, know how to access them, be eligible to receive them, and perceive that these services will actually help them.

 Families at risk for child abuse and neglect need a sense of positive community. They need someone they can call when a child is sick and in need of medicine or when childcare falls through at the last minute. They need someone who is further along in the parenting or life journey to lend them a word of advice or a helping hand. They need emotional support—someone to care, trust, and think well of them, someone to offer empathy or a different perspective. They need informational support—how to help their baby to sleep through the night or where to go for low-cost vaccinations. And they need someone who can provide practical help, such as assistance with childcare, transportation, or other basic tasks of day-to-day life.

That's a whole lot that needs to be in place for a family to have adequate social support. Also, trust is a big issue. Many parents are reluctant to ask for help because they have been taken advantage of or lied to in the past, or promises have not been kept. Do all you can to be respectful and patient when interacting with families. Unless you've walked in their shoes, you don't really know what they've been through or what they need. And if you say you're going to do something, by all means, do it.

More than any other area, our faith communities have a lot to offer families in the area of social support. Most of our faith communities have positive parenting models: we have people of all generations. We even have committees that are charged with outreach. Will we have the guts to reach out? Will we help lonely parents? Will we be a friend and lend a hand? I believe that if we knew how big a difference that could really make for a family or a child, we would do it.

Jesus' family

Let's think about the earthly family into which Jesus was born. Looking at the first two chapters of both Matthew and Luke, we find many indicators of risk and protection. In twenty-first century standards Mary was a poor, young, single mother who was in relationship with a much older man. When she was nearing her due date, she and her boyfriend commenced on a long, difficult trip. At the birth of Jesus, the family was homeless in an unfamiliar land with no healthcare, no support of family, friends, or church community. The only baby shower was thrown by shepherds and wise men. And while Jesus was still young, King Herod sought to kill him, his family became refugees in Egypt, and, later still, he was left behind in Jerusalem.

Parents need to know that services are there, know how to access them, be eligible to receive them, and perceive that these services will actually help them.

Some of these factors were quite typical for families in that day. And yes, Mary was in a *very* committed relationship. Nevertheless, there were many risk factors present—some of which were personal to the family and some of which were brought to them by their environment.

At the same time, Joseph and Mary had a lot of strengths. They each had faith in God; they were chosen and called by God to their parental roles. They followed God's guidance in naming, protecting, and raising their son. Their basic needs for food, shelter, and clothing were met. They had strong social support during the pregnancy and during much of Jesus' childhood (think of the caravan of people traveling to Jerusalem).

Which of us would not like this said about our son or daughter: "The child grew up healthy and strong. He was filled with wisdom, and God's favor was on him" (Luke 2:40)?

Whether we work through personal relationships or through larger system changes, we can make a positive impact on families. By so doing, we help prevent child abuse and neglect for this generation and for generations to come.

Discussion Questions

1. Look up Matthew 1–2 and Luke 1–2. What specific risk and protective factors do you identify in Jesus' earthly family? Fill in a grid similar to the one below.

	Risk Factors	Protective Factors
While Mary was pregnant with Jesus		
When Jesus was born		
When Jesus was young		

2. What are some of the major risk factors for child abuse and neglect in your community?
3. What do you think are some of the causes of poverty? What can the church do to help families out of poverty?
4. Do you know families who have experienced domestic violence or substance abuse? What was the effect on the children?
5. Do you know an adult who had to be resilient as a child? What was this experience like for this person?
6. What have been your experiences with parenting classes—positive and negative?
7. To what degree does your church offer social support to its members? In what ways does it also offer social support to families outside the church?

Action Items

1. Call a local domestic violence agency, request information, and ask what your church can do to help. To find a domestic violence shelter in the United States, contact the National Domestic Violence Hotline, 1-800-799-SAFE or www.ndvh.org. In Canada, contact Shelternet, www.shelternet.ca/en, or the Religion and Violence e-Learning (Rave) project, www.theraveproject.com/index.php/help/shelter_map/canada.

2. Call a local agency that provides substance abuse treatment, request information, and ask what your church can do to help. In the United States, contact the Substance Abuse and Mental Health Services Administration (SAMHSA), www.findtreatment.samhsa.gov. In Canada, contact the Canadian Centre on Substance Abuse, www.ccsa.ca

3. Find parenting classes available in your community. Call to see if they need help with childcare or transportation.

4. Research parenting curricula that your church could use in teaching parenting (see appendix 1).

5. Think of a family you know that has a child with a disability. Contact this family and ask what you can do to be helpful this week. Maybe you can take a meal, provide transportation, or lend a listening ear.

Chapter 9

Offenders

Beware of false prophets who come disguised as harmless sheep but are really vicious wolves.

—*Matthew 7:15*

We could probably think of more pleasant topics to discuss than offenders of child abuse and neglect. Nevertheless, if we are to keep children safe, we must look in the face of those from whom we must keep them safe.

We must first look in the mirror. Yes, we must each accept the harsh reality that we have the potential to hurt a child. We're probably not going to hurt a child intentionally. But depending on our background, our circumstances, our day, we have the potential to do so. We are not immune.

When I present this in class, my young adult students often take great offense at my comments. "No, Dr. Harder, I could never hurt a child!" It is interesting that I have never gotten this response from someone who is a parent. In the best of times, parenting is hard. But how often do we live in the best of times?

Do not hear me justifying abusive behavior. I am only asking that before we move to judge the behavior of others, we first examine our own thoughts and behaviors (the log in our own eye). It is only by the grace of God that I was born into a nurturing family and not an abusive one. It is by the grace of God that I have strong social support, am not addicted to drugs or alcohol, and have many positive parenting role models.

Perhaps you too were born into a family like Timothy in the Bible. In 2 Timothy 1:5, we read about the positive influence that Timothy's mother and grandmother had on his spiritual growth. Just a few verses earlier (v. 2), Paul called Timothy, "my dear son." Timothy was blessed by caring, strong people of varying generations.

Those of us blessed with loving, nurturing families must remember not to make snap or harsh judgments of others, especially when their backgrounds are different from our own.

The overarching mandate for all of us is that we keep children safe. We must not be in denial that child abuse and neglect happens, and so we must not be in denial that offenders are around us. Also—and I cannot emphasize this enough—offenders do not have horns growing out of their heads. They may be disguised like "harmless sheep" when really they are "vicious wolves" (Matthew 7:15). In other words, an offender does not often look scary physically, but rather looks harmless and otherwise acts quite normally. In fact, an offender may be quite charming. An offender may be a respected leader in your church or community.

There is not a simple list of characteristics that help us identify a potential or current offender. As shown below, offenders are usually parents of their victims (80 percent of the time). Of offending parents, they are biological parents nearly all of the time (91 percent). Most often, it is not the stranger jumping out from a dark alley and grabbing our children.

Just over half of offenders (57 percent) are women rather than men. Most offenders are between the ages of twenty and forty years, but adolescents are a growing group of offenders. In 2007, the median age for female offenders was thirty-one, and the median age for male offenders was thirty-four.[1] The racial distribution of offenders was similar to that of victims. That said, the characteristics of an offender vary greatly, especially between types of abuse and neglect.

Relationship of Offenders to Victims

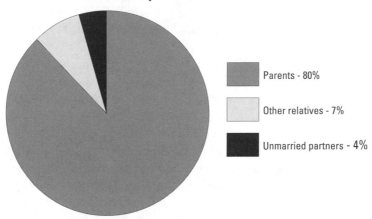

- Parents - 80%
- Other relatives - 7%
- Unmarried partners - 4%

Gender of Offenders

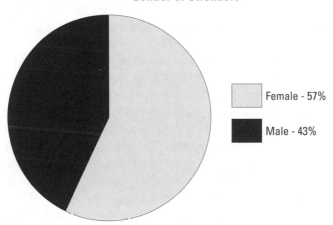

- Female - 57%
- Male - 43%

Characteristics of offenders of child neglect

Rates of child neglect correlate strongly with those of poverty, and so the characteristics of these parents are also similar to those in poverty: single mothers with multiple children who are close in age. In one study, communities with the highest rates of poverty had eighteen times more reports of neglect than did communities with the lowest rates of poverty.[2] Families with four or more children were also twice or three times more likely to neglect their children.[3] Parents who have their children when they are in their teens are consistently at a greater risk for neglecting their children, especially if a child was born prematurely. Most neglectful parents are socially isolated. They are more likely to be depressed, act impulsively, and have low self-esteem, low ability to be empathetic, and high stress.

As faith communities, we must do all we can to confront poverty and social isolation so we can protect children.

Neglectful parents typically interact less with their children, and when they do interact, it is less positive. They issue more commands and engage in verbal aggression with their children. They show less affection for their children, are less warm, and spend less time playing with them. Offenders of child neglect are not typically a threat to children outside their own family.

Helping neglectful families is very challenging, and change does not come overnight. Neglect, like poverty, is often generational and becomes a part of a family's culture. Helping these types of parents through the provision of concrete resources is a great step but is not enough. Yes, they need food, housing, and childcare, but they also need a friend, positive role models, and help with education, employment, housing, healthcare, and budgeting. Many of these families also struggle with substance abuse, mental health, and domestic violence.

Presented with this type of parent, how do you want to respond? How can we prevent child neglect? Remember that neglect accounts for more than half of abuse and neglect cases in the United States and nearly one-third of cases in Canada.

The short- and long-term effects of neglect on a child are great. As faith communities, we must do all we can to confront poverty and social isolation so we can protect these children. This is a huge and complex problem facing North America and each of our communities, and we must rise up to confront it. We must reach out to neglectful parents in a way that is helpful and not judgmental—in a way that preserves dignity and self-determination, and yet protects the most vulnerable, the children.

Characteristics of offenders of child physical abuse

Like offenders of all types of abuse and neglect, offenders of child physical abuse vary considerably. In general, offenders of physical abuse are a bit younger and their first child was often born when the parent was a teen. In the United States offenders are female slightly more often (56 percent) than they are male (43 percent), probably because women spend more time in caretaking of children than do men.

Most physical abuse is done by a child's biological parents (85 percent). Children living in single-parent families are much more at risk (63 percent) than children living in two-parent families, probably due to the poverty and stress often associated with single-parent families. Of family-related physical assaults on children reported to the police in Canada in 2007, 71 percent were committed by males (44 percent by fathers, 13 percent by brothers, and 10 percent by male extended family members).[4]

As you might guess, offenders of physical abuse typically have a hard time controlling their anger, they are hostile, have a low frustration tolerance, are depressed, have low self-esteem, abuse substances, have deficits in empathy, have poor problem-solving skills, and/or are rigid. They typically experience a lot of anxiety and stress and are under personal distress. They are likely to be isolated from family and friends, experiencing conflict with their spouse, and engaging in negative family interactions. Physically abusive parents have unrealistic expectations and negative perceptions of their children. They spend less time interacting with their children, and when they do interact, it is highly directive, critical, and controlling.

Do you know someone who fits these characteristics? Perhaps it describes your own parent or yourself. Parenting education classes can be helpful, especially classes that teach child development and skills related to coping, anger management, and problem solving. We can also help these families by easing the stress in the home.

Children in physically abusive homes live in constant fear and are very vulnerable to life-threatening injuries. When a child has unusual bruises or cuts, expresses or displays fear of going home, or haltingly tells us about the abuse going on at home, we must respond. We must report our concerns to the authorities and be ready to help.

Characteristics of offenders of child emotional abuse

Compared to other types of abuse or neglect, we don't know as much about offenders of emotional abuse. We do know that emotional abuse often accompanies other types of abuse and neglect, and the effects to children are devastating. Similar to the offenders of other types of abuse or neglect, the offenders of emotional abuse are most often a parent, and most often the mother. These parents frequently experience stress in other areas of their lives, are socially isolated, have difficulty with social interactions, and have poor problem-solving skills. One difference is that a greater proportion of offenders of emotional abuse are Caucasian rather than other races.

While less is known about the offender of child emotional abuse, perhaps this is the type of abuse that many of us struggle with. When we acknowledge the sensitivity of our children and their concrete perceptions, we realize that the things we say (or yell) do hurt children.

When we encounter a parent screaming at a child in the grocery store or any public place, we must be creative in finding a way to deflect that parent's attention without making things worse for the child or putting ourselves in harm's way. Often by showing understanding and empathy, we can defuse a situation. However, emotional abuse is more likely to be displayed at home or other non-public places, and then we must find other ways to discover and intervene on behalf of the child.

Characteristics of offenders of child sexual abuse

Of all types of offenders, the sex offender is probably the one that frightens us the most. Rightfully so, this type of offender preys on children in many places (not just the home), and our churches are often ideal places for an offender to gain access to children. Regardless of the size or location of our church, we may be inadvertently providing offenders with easy access to children.

Offenders of sexual abuse are often known to the child and family and gain access to the child outside the home in places like playgrounds, cars, homes, campgrounds, and, yes, in church basements, Sunday school rooms, and youth rooms. We must take a hard look at our churches—more specifically our facilities, our policies, our beliefs—and consider how they may set up a child for abuse. We need to examine our programs, especially those that are less formal or less organized, and see how they may leave our children vulnerable to abuse.

Offenders of sexual abuse are sometimes unknown to the child and family. Those of us in large churches may not be as good at noticing a stranger when one walks in our door and down our hallways. But then again, those of us in large churches may have more resources and be more likely to have abuse prevention policies and to require background checks of all individuals who work with children.

Those of us in small churches may be quicker to notice a stranger, but we probably don't have as many resources available to us, don't have an abuse prevention policy, and are aghast at the idea of requiring background checks.

Folks in small churches are often like family to one another.

While this is great, it can also be the breeding ground for an offender to have access to children without anyone raising concerns.

Sex offenders are different from other types of offenders in several ways. First, most sex offenders are male (87 percent in the United States). Some females, however, do commit sexual offenses—a woman may prey on a child or may act as an accomplice to a male. More often than not, sex offenders are known to the child but may or may not be biologically related to the child. In the United States, nearly half of sex offenses (40 percent) are by acquaintances, friends, or family friends; 37 percent by a biological parent, and 23 percent by a stepparent or parent's partner.[5]

As faith communities, we must be especially alert to the possibility of sexual abuse and do all we can to protect children.

One characteristic that varies considerably is age; in fact, adolescents represent 40 percent of all offenders. Sex offenders may be young, middle aged, or older. Most sex offenders developed their deviant sexual interests prior to age eighteen and experienced sexual abuse as children themselves.

So how can we keep our children safe from sex offenders? There are certainly many things we can do. We are not helpless in protecting our children.

The most important thing is not to be in denial that sexual abuse happens. While it's not any fun to be suspicious, we still must be very cautious when it comes to allowing someone to be alone with our children. It is our responsibility as adults to protect children. We can provide children with education on sexual abuse, help them to learn ways of saying no, and encourage them to tell us if an adult touches them or shows them things that are confusing or upsetting. But we cannot depend on children to protect themselves.

The approaches of an offender are too complex and too

varied for us to expect our children to be able to recognize inappropriate behavior and respond appropriately. The offender may spend years in grooming and gaining access to the child, both physically and emotionally. The offender may threaten that if a child doesn't cooperate, something bad will happen. The offender may shower the child with gifts and praise, leading the child to believe that she likes the sexual attention and is needed by the offender. As adults, parents, and churches, we must be the ones to stop the sex offender.

This stance raises the question of whether we as Christians can offer forgiveness to a child sex offender. The answer is yes. But that doesn't mean we grant offenders access to children. You will not find someone in a bar who is serious about overcoming an addiction to alcohol. You will not find someone in a casino who is working to overcome an addiction to gambling.

The same goes for sex offenders. They should not be placed in a position of temptation, especially when their object of addiction is a child. If the offender is serious about overcoming deviant sexual behaviors, then the offender will welcome our help in staying away from children and/or situations that may be difficult. We can say to the previous offender, "Prove by the way you live that you have repented of your sins and turned to God" (Matthew 3:8).

You or your church may want to participate in a Circles of Support and Accountability (CoSA) program or start one in your community. CoSA programs link community volunteers with individuals who have a history of sexual offense to provide support to the individual and help ensure safety for the community. The main goal of this program is to reduce victimization. Contact information for this program in both the United States and Canadian can be found under "Helpful Organizations" in the back of this book.

You might ask, "What would Jesus do?" Jesus forgave people for their behaviors, and called them to right behavior. All actions have consequences. The consequence for someone sexually offending a child is that the perpetrator must not be given opportunity to offend again.

All actions have consequences. The consequence for someone sexually offending a child is that the perpetrator must not be given opportunity to offend again.

When it comes to a child abuse offender, the church often feels torn between accepting and forgiving the sinner while also protecting and valuing the children. For the sake of our children, child safety must be considered the higher priority. Satisfactory alternatives can be found for the offender to enter into worship and fellowship without putting a child at risk.

Churches and pastors should turn to denominational leaders or conference ministers for assistance in knowing how to respond to a child abuse offender. If the offender is still in treatment for previous offenses, the church can communicate with the treatment provider to determine the best ways to keep children in your church safe.

Discussion Questions

1. Describe a time when it was particularly difficult for you to be patient and loving toward a child. What did you need at that time?
2. What would it take for you to believe that someone is a child sex offender?
3. If a parent in your small group is neglecting his child (physical neglect or neglectful supervision), what could you say to this person? What would you actually say? What would you want to do? What would you actually do?
   a. What if this parent was physically abusing a child?
   b. Emotionally abusing a child?
   c. Sexually abusing a child?
4. Why do you think we are more horrified by sexual abuse than by other types of abuse or neglect?
5. What should the church's response be to each type of offender?

6. Which types of abuse do you think are most important for your church to work toward ending?

Action Items

1. Find the list of sex offenders in the community around your church and your home. In the United States see National Alert Registry [nominal fee]: www.nationalalertregistry.com or Family Watch Dog: www.familywatchdog.us). In Canada, check with your local authorities to see if a list of convicted sex offenders is available for your community. It is important to be aware of the presence of these individuals but not to ostracize them.
2. Contact a local program that serves children or families with low incomes. Learn about the services and volunteer opportunities at the program.
3. Make a list of healthy ways for you to handle anger.
4. Find or make a poster that helps children identify and express their feelings. Give these posters to families in your church and neighborhood.
5. Read one of the Gospels and note how Jesus responded to people who had sinned.

Chapter 10

Ending Child Abuse and Neglect in our Communities

Love your neighbor as yourself.

—Matthew 22:39

We are not powerless. As faith communities, we can do so much to end child abuse and neglect in the communities where we live and work. We can "give justice to the poor and the orphan, uphold the rights of the oppressed and the destitute. Rescue the poor and helpless" (Psalm 82:3-4a).

A first step is to acknowledge that abuse exists and that it exists in our own communities. We must learn to recognize different types of child abuse or neglect and the risk and protective factors for children and families. Then we must move past brain work and into feet and hands work. In big ways and small ways, we must act. Children need our protection; they need us to speak up for them, to act on their behalf. A child's future can be shattered by abuse and neglect, or a child's future can be redeemed or preserved—you can make the difference.

I attended a conference recently in which we were encouraged to be "everyday heroes" for children. The keynote speaker shared her story of horrendous sexual abuse as a child but gave us hope and purpose as she spoke of the protection offered by an elderly neighbor. The neighbor was not able to stop the abuse, but by speaking and embodying God's love, she was able to help this child see that the abuse was not her fault, find ways to protect herself, and, most of all, to rise above her difficult circumstances.

You too can make a huge difference to a child by offering your friendship, a listening ear as you make cookies together, a kind heart as you play ball at the park. Every child needs someone to trust, someone who can be there. If a parent is not able to do this, then you can offer this as a friend, neighbor, teacher, or coach. Do not underestimate the power of relationships. We may not be able to stop the bull from charging, but we can lessen the blow, wrap the wounds, and perhaps get the child out of the arena. All children seek attention and love—you can offer this, can't you?

A child's future can be shattered by abuse and neglect, or a child's future can be redeemed or preserved— you can make the difference.

Likewise, families need everyday heroes—someone to offer help when the going gets rough. They don't need our judgment or our scorn; they need a hand. Many families will resist a handout, but we can offer help in ways that preserve dignity and empower them to positive action. Families have strengths—they have positive things going for them—and we must capitalize on these strengths and help families rise above their difficulties.

The church's role in ending child abuse in our communities:

- Provide concrete resources
- Offer social support
- Get involved in the community
- Report abuse and neglect

Provide concrete resources

 As faith communities, we can make a significant dent in child neglect by offering concrete resources to the families in our communities. Through food and clothing pantries, rental and utility assistance, job training and assistance, childcare, medical and dental clinics, we can help families in poverty to keep from sinking into neglect.

Like in the parable of the great feast, we can "go quickly into the streets and alleys of the town and invite the poor, the crippled, the blind, and the lame" (Luke 14:21). We can follow the examples of many in the Bible who gave generously to the poor. Tabitha (also known as Dorcas) was "always doing kind things for others and helping the poor" (Acts 9:36). Cornelius gave gifts to the poor (Acts 10:4), as did Paul (Acts 24:17) and the people of Macedonia and Achaia (Romans 15:25-28).

Many community agencies depend on the faith community to provide critical concrete resources to families. In recent years, many community food pantries have lost funding and had to close their doors; others are open for fewer hours and restrict whom they will serve. While you may not consider these activities as child abuse prevention, service providers who work directly with families certainly do, and they appreciate your hard work and generosity.

The role churches play in providing food and clothing is critical and should not be understated. Concrete resources are getting more and more difficult for poor families to access. As unemployment rates mount and costs for food, housing, healthcare, and childcare skyrocket, more and more families need to access this kind of help. For many, the wages they earn just can't stretch far enough, especially when it comes to meeting the needs of children who can have insatiable appetites and who outgrow their clothes and shoes so quickly.

The task of running a food pantry or second-hand clothing store requires skills that many church members possess.

With volunteer help such a resource can operate on a very lean budget. Many churches have members who are not interested or able to be employed but would be very happy to contribute a few hours a week to stocking shelves in a food pantry or running the cash register at a second-hand clothing store. Do not underestimate the contribution this provides in strengthening families and protecting children.

Depending on the size of our churches and the resources available to us, we can offer this kind of help ourselves. Or, we can combine our resources with other churches or already existing organizations to strengthen current programs and make them more accessible for the families who need them. Accessibility includes location, hours, and facilities. These kinds of services must be offered in safe locations and accessible by car or bus. The hours open must allow parents to work and still access services. Facilities must be clean, safe, and welcoming for all, including those with physical disabilities. Paperwork and services must be offered in the languages families speak.

We must find ways to preserve dignity in families. We may allow a low-income family to pay a small amount for items, like Christmas or birthday gifts for their children. At the very least, we can allow families more choice in what they receive. We can also invite families to volunteer their time so that more people can be served.

While designed to help neglectful families, these services can also strengthen families who are struggling with other types of abuse as well as families who are mired in poverty. Many of our churches are already contributing to similar programs. By realizing the positive impact these services can have on protecting children, energy and resources for these types of ministries can be increased.

Offer social support

One of the biggest risk factors for all types of child abuse and neglect is isolation. Families who do not have formal or infor-

mal supports in place can quickly fall to pieces when tough times come. Can you imagine not having a friend to call when you need to talk, not having anyone to turn to when you need to run to work for a few hours and cannot take your child, or wanting to celebrate a new job and not having anyone to go out with? Like Jesus in the Garden of Gethsemane (Matthew 26:38), we desire the presence and support of others, especially when we hit rough times. The church has a lot to offer in the way of emotional support if people in the church are willing to reach out and invest in new relationships.

Many families at risk would benefit from a friend, a role model, someone to care about them and listen to them. Research shows that when someone takes the time to visit and form a relationship with an at risk family, it greatly reduces the likelihood of abuse in that family. This is especially true for young, low-income single mothers when their first child is born.

While community and governmental organizations would like to provide home visitation and mentoring programs, when it comes right down to it, the funding for these programs usually gets cut in favor of funding for helping those families who are already in the system (who have already abused their children). The church could play a significant role in partnering with a hospital or daycare and helping new families through those first critical months and years of parenthood. Families with preschool and school-age children would also benefit from a mentor or regular home visitor. Formal or informal, your visits can make a difference with a family through your genuine, nonjudgmental friendship.

Most churches help only those families within their congregation. Depending on their level of outreach, many churches are relatively isolated—busy with their own activities, their own challenges, and safe in their predictable ways of doing things.

When I ask service providers who work one-on-one with

families at risk for abuse, they say that very few of their families are connected with a church.

Many families at risk would benefit from a friend, a role model, someone to care about them and listen to them.

So while the church may learn to protect its own children and families, what about the children and families who do not or will not come to your building? Let's face it, bringing families with issues into our congregation may be unsettling. It may jar us a bit. It may cause us to think about things in new ways, and to reach out in ways that are new and uncomfortable to us.

Children who have experienced abuse or neglect or are at risk for abuse or neglect may not be able to conform to our rules and certainly may not be able to sit still and quiet during a children's service or worship service. Is your church ready to welcome these children? Does Jesus love these children? Should we just hope that someone else—the church down the street, the school, the detention center—will take care of these kids?

If you value families with both children and parents, then you will need to welcome the parents of these kids as well. These parents will have incredible gifts to offer your congregation, but if they are going through difficult times, these talents may be buried under mental health issues, addictions, poor decision-making, and unpredictability. Are you willing to stand by them, to listen to them, to help them through this time of crisis, perpetual crisis perhaps, to bring them back to the place of wholeness that God desires for them? Will you be Christ to them?

Most service providers I have spoken with express considerable reservation in referring an at risk family to a church for help. On one hand, they know some churches to be very responsive and helpful to families. If they know the pastor well and feel that the church would be helpful to the family, they definitely encourage the family to be in contact with the church. On the other hand, they know some churches to be judgmental and condoning of power imbalances in families. They are concerned that faith communities are judgmental of certain kinds of families and try to proselytize, which in their terms is a coercive and disrespectful action.

If a family reports previous involvement or interest in a church, most professionals say they encourage the family to seek help from that church. However, if the family or individual does not mention any connection to a church, the professional will not likely encourage one. To their credit, more and more community programs are including questions about religious preferences on their assessment forms, so hopefully the door to collaboration between churches and community professionals is swinging further open.

Get involved in the community

 Community agencies need not only your financial contributions, but also your time, knowledge, and skills. Perhaps you can give of your time one evening a week or one Saturday a month to help at a local community program. Perhaps you have expertise in financial management or marketing and can serve on the board of an organization. Perhaps you can become a mentor for a child or a partner for a homeless or refugee family. Maybe you can answer phones or stock shelves. Most schools would welcome a couple hours of your time to read to children, work in the library, or plan a classroom party.

There is so much to do; where do we start? We can't do it all. That's right—none of us as individuals or churches can do it all, but we can each do something. We must not be paralyzed by indecision or by the enormity of the task. We can start small and do the things we can, the things we do best. God calls us to be faithful with what we have, and then we may be entrusted with more. You will never be able to predict or measure the extent of your work, nor know all the lives you have touched. I believe making a positive difference in one child's life, in one family, is significant. Don't you?

You can also expect changes in yourself, in your passions, perhaps in the direction of your life. Earlier in my life, I was a secretary. In all humbleness, I was a good secretary. But through volunteering at a local program for abused children, I realized that I could do more.

My husband and I began going to a residential home for children every Thursday evening, helping a group of girls, ages six to twelve, with their homework, playing on the playground with them, and helping to move them through their evening routine. We quickly began to feel an affinity for these girls and wanted

You will never be able to predict or measure the extent of your work, nor know all the lives you have touched.

to do more for them. We got approved so we could take them to our home for visits when they were not able to do the same with their parents. We then became a foster family for a couple girls who especially touched our hearts.

My husband and I were forever changed by our experiences with these young girls. As a result, I returned to school to become a social worker, and my life is now full in ways I'd never imagined possible. I am happy with the paths God has shown me to help others. Volunteering in a community program and taking the risk to build relationships with those in need forever changed my life; I pray that, in some way, I have been an everyday hero for many.

Even if you don't have time to volunteer in a community agency or school, I urge you to visit them and get to know the services they offer and the people who work there. You will be much better equipped to help other people access services in the community if you have visited these agencies yourself.

Another idea that can work very well is to invite service providers to speak to your church, class, or small group. They have a wealth of information to share with you. It's not until we get to know community agencies and the people who work there that we can effectively collaborate with them.

Report child abuse and neglect

Another important step is for us to report our suspicions of child abuse and neglect to the authorities. In the United States make reports to either Child Protective Services (CPS) or the police. In Canada check with your local CPS office to determine if abuse is to be reported there or to the police. (In First Nations communities report suspected abuse to First Nations Child and Family Service Agencies.) You may ask: how does reporting abuse help to prevent child abuse and neglect? The goals of CPS are to keep children safe and to strengthen families. Similarly, the police seek to ensure public safety.

We may be tempted to think that the role of CPS is to remove children from homes, which is what we often read about in the newspaper. That is an unfortunate part of its job. But much more often CPS works to make families and homes safe places for children. This includes investigating concerns and connecting families with services like parent education, concrete resources, and counselors. Ultimately, it is not the sole responsibility of CPS to protect children; it is ours. Through our tax money CPS is able to focus time, expertise, and energy to help us with this task. But CPS cannot do it without us. And we cannot do it without them.

CPS works in cooperation with local police and the courts. CPS responds to reports of abuse or neglect when the alleged offender is a parent or caretaker. Depending on where you live, police respond to reports of abuse or neglect when the alleged offender is a non-family member, friend, or stranger to the child. Legal entities, such as police and the courts, must be involved for a child to be removed from a home and for an arrest to be made and prosecution pursued.

Depending on the size of your community, CPS and the police work together to respond to reports of child abuse and neglect. You can call one or the other, and they will communicate with each other as needed. In the United States, the National Child Abuse Hotline number is 1-800-4ACHILD (1-800-422-4453).

Sometimes as faith communities, we are reluctant to work with the authorities (CPS or police). Too often, I have heard of churches that concealed abuse, thinking they could handle it themselves. Consequently, children languish without help, and alleged offenders move on to hurt more children. The job of investigating alleged abuse or neglect and stopping the bad guys is not what many of us are trained or otherwise prepared to do. All investigative work must be left to the authorities. The complexities of the task are enormous.

Reporting suspected abuse may be what it takes to protect a child.

As faith communities, we need to partner with professional organizations to end child abuse and neglect. No one entity can do it alone—we need to work together. It may help to realize that many CPS workers and police officers are members of faith communities themselves and entered into their profession because of their passion to protect children.

Reporting our suspicions is part of the work of ending child abuse and neglect because it aims to stop the abuse in its tracks and turn things around for the family and child. Reporting suspected abuse may be what it takes to protect a child in the short- and long-term. Reporting abuse may be what it takes for an offender to get the treatment needed to stop hurting more children.

Reporting abuse to the authorities is also the law. In nearly all states in the United States and provinces and territories in Canada, all adults are required by law to report suspected child abuse. The remaining states require professionals (including ministers/priests) to report and encourage everyone else to do so. We do not need to be 100 percent confident in order to report child abuse and neglect; we just need to have reasonable concern.

Many communities have a child advocacy center, which houses professionals and provides investigation, case management, medical, therapy, and legal services—all in one child-friendly place. This approach seems to do the least harm to the child who has been victimized by abuse and neglect. When we ask a child to repeatedly tell her story, often to people who are strangers to her, not only does her story change, but she is re-victimized.

A child advocacy center allows for a child to be interviewed once by a forensic interviewer who is trained in talking with children, as well as in legal requirements. A forensic interviewer would know, for example, to inquire further when a child states, "My papa puts his peepee in my peepee," and figure out whether the child is talking about blatant sexual abuse or whether the child is talking about he and his father peeing in the same toilet without flushing in between.

When making a report to the authorities, whether it is CPS or the police, we must be prepared to relate as much information as we can. They will want to know the name, gender, age (including date of birth) of the child, and where this child can be located (addresses for home, school, childcare). They will want the same information for parents and caretakers, and other siblings. (You may, however, report even if you don't have all this information.)

Be prepared to provide as much concrete information as you can about what you saw or what you were told, including dates and detailed descriptions. If you're reporting because you saw welts on the back of a child's legs, you will want to report exactly where the welts were (approximate number of inches from the knees or buttocks), how long they were, what color they were, and what the child said they came from. It is always a great idea to keep notes on what you have seen, including the date and precise description. Sometimes little things don't look like much until they start adding up or something bigger happens.

For example, you can report that an eight-year-old neighbor girl, Cindy, came to your house two weeks ago (on September 8), and you observed that she was walking peculiarly. When you asked her, she said she had something in her shoes. On September 13 you heard Cindy's father yelling at her; when you stepped out on your porch, you saw that he was holding a belt in his hand. Then on September 25 you saw five-inch long bright red welts on the backs of Cindy's legs, about halfway between her knees and her buttocks. When you asked her what happened, she said that she got a sunburn. This final incident needs to be reported, using your notes from September 8 and 13 as your backup.

It is important that you not probe the child for information. Ask open-ended questions, such as: "Tell me more about that." Or simply, "I'm listening." Project Harmony, a child advocacy agency in Omaha, Nebraska, has developed a minimal facts interview, which includes asking the child these questions:

1. What happened?
2. When did (the abuse) happen?
3. Who did it? (Is _____ a grown-up or a kid?)
4. Does this person live or stay in your home?[1]

Allow the child to talk with you and share what he wishes. Respond calmly and warmly to the child. If you react with visible shock, he may think he did something wrong, compounding the feelings that he has done something wrong to cause the abuse or neglect. If you react with disbelief, the child may think you don't believe him, and may stop talk-ing—he may not get up the nerve to tell someone else. Make careful observations of both what you see and hear, taking note of not only how the child appears, but also how he behaves. Be sure not to proceed any further with questioning the child; leave the work of investigation to the authorities.

The child may ask you not to tell anyone what happened—to keep it a secret. Tell the child how brave he is to tell what happened and how good it is he told you. Reassure the child that he is not in trouble and did not do anything wrong. Then kindly explain that you will need to tell the authorities so this doesn't happen again. Explore with the child ways he can be safe.

When discussing abuse they have experienced, children's

words and actions may be incongruent. For example, they may giggle while telling you about how someone hurt them, or they may show no emotion whatsoever. Take seriously what a child tells you—young children in particular rarely lie about such matters.

Make sure the child is safe, and report the abuse to the authorities as soon as possible. If you delay in making the report, not only may you be putting the child at further risk of abuse or neglect, but any physical effects of the abuse may heal. Also, delays in making reports may deny the child of needed medical care.

In order for CPS or the police to substantiate (determine) that abuse has occurred, they need evidence. Evidence in cases of child abuse and neglect include the child's testimony (if available); marks on the child; and supporting evidence from others, including reports of what the child has said, or the child's behavior.

Including your name and contact information when you report abuse is not required, but encouraged. By law, CPS or the police cannot give your name to the family—this would only come up if the case were to go to court. Giving your name allows CPS or the police to let you know the outcome of their investigation as well as to seek more information, if needed. If the alleged abuse is found to be untrue by CPS or the police, the case is closed, and you as the reporter are not held liable, as you were reporting "in good faith." (See appendix 2.)

Some of us may refrain from reporting suspected abuse to CPS or the police because we believe the system is broken, will not respond, or will not be helpful to the child. It is true that sometimes CPS and the police do not do the right thing, but more often than not they are constrained by the limited evidence we give them, or they lack adequate resources to do what we expect of them.

Another way we as faith communities can work to end child abuse and neglect is to work at the macro level. We can write to our legislators and let them know our hopes, dreams, and concerns for children and families in our community. We can influ-

---

Reporting Suspected Abuse or Neglect

1. Attend to the child's immediate safety, if needed.

2. Make notes of your concerns, including what you've heard and seen.

3. If within your church, speak to a child protection team member or someone who can provide support or guidance.

4. Report the following to CPS or the police as soon as possible:
    a. child's name, gender, age, address, school or childcare, if available
    b. what the child said, if anything
    c. what you observed about the child, the child's family, and/or the child's surroundings
    d. your concerns
    e. your name and phone number (optional; it will not be shared with the child or family)

5. Continue to attend to the child's safety as well as the safety of any other children who may be affected.

---

ence policy by going to meetings and informing our legislators of our concerns. We are not powerless. Children in our families and communities need us to hear and see them, and to be their voice. Remember, when we offer food to the hungry, drink to the thirsty, invite the stranger into our home, clothe the naked, care for the sick, and visit those in prison, we may be serving the Lord himself (Matthew 25:34-46).

Discussion Questions

1. In your childhood, who was an everyday hero for you? What did this person do? How did this affect you?
2. What kinds of concrete services are you or your church already providing children? Do you think this plays a role in preventing child abuse? If so, how?
3. Share experiences of reporting child abuse (if any). What was this like for you?
4. Have you ever suspected child abuse or neglect but did not report it? What stopped you?
5. How could your church more effectively reach at risk families in your community?

Action Items

1. Make a list of agencies where you can refer families for food, shelter, rent or utility assistance, childcare, and education/job training. Include the name of the agency, address, and phone number. Share this list with your pastor.
2. Call your local CPS office or police unit and invite someone to speak to your church or group about child abuse.
3. Contact a local hospital and learn what services are available for new parents.
4. Meet or talk with a neighbor this week.
5. Make announcements at your church about the needs of agencies in your community—needs either for volunteers or for donated items.
6. Make refrigerator magnets or business cards with the phone number for reporting child abuse. Give to everyone in your church (or group).

Chapter 11

Ending Child Abuse and Neglect in our Churches

Let the children come to me. Don't stop them! For the Kingdom of God belongs to those who are like these children.
—Mark 10:14

"**M**y attitude is that no kid in our church is going to be hurt on my watch, so to speak. We're going to make sure that the kids are protected." These sincere words from a pastor echo the hope and determination of most church leaders. Another pastor we interviewed said that his prayer at the end of the day is that nothing he has done or said has caused damage to anyone. I think those who teach children and youth would say the same thing. Like Eli caring for boy Samuel in the temple (1 Samuel 3), we desire to be patient and good listeners, providing loving care and wise instruction to children.

In our churches, we never want to do harm, and what frightens us, in all honesty, is that we realize we probably will hurt someone. Our prayer, therefore, is that the harm we do will be minimal and reversible. The harm done by child abuse and neglect is not minimal, and the wounds left behind, whether physical or emotional, are often deep.

On one hand, we need to protect the children in our churches from someone who may hurt them with words or actions. On the other hand, and very relevant for our churches today, we must protect the children in our churches from the pain they may experience from our inaction.

For whatever reason, many churches do not take needed steps to protect the children in their watch, and it is quite likely that these children will be hurt by this lack of action and attention. Whether this inaction is intentional or not does not matter to the child who has become a victim.

If a church intentionally does not protect a child, the child's hurt is multiplied—she is hurt first by the offender and then re-victimized by the church. Allowing an offender to remain in good standing in the church, not believing the child, or rushing all parties to forgiveness and reconciliation re-victimizes the child and make the wounds fester and ooze rather than giving them opportunity to heal.

One pastor stated, "There is a large spectrum of things to be done, but procrastination and doing nothing is not it. And it would not go over well with me to know that our children had been hurt."

Our churches desire to do good, to be God's hand of healing and restoration in the world. The church must actively work to protect children within its programs and communities.

In speaking with church leaders, we learned that churches lie on a very long continuum between those who are very protective of children and those who are not. No church leader has ever told me, "No, it is not a priority for us to protect children from child abuse and neglect." Rather, a church leader sends silent messages that children's safety is not a priority: the church does not have a child abuse policy, would not report suspected child abuse to the authorities, and is not informed of the signs of child abuse. These churches value the sovereignty of the family more than they value children, or they are more concerned with maintaining and restoring relationships to the neglect of accountability.

Some churches are just not well-informed. For these, I can

hope that education on the reality of child abuse and neglect will move them to action, so that a child does not have to be hurt and make an outcry to move them into protective mode. Some churches I've spoken with admitted to past incidents of child abuse they did not report and that did not end well, and still they remain in complacency. Many churches unwilling to protect their children fear loss of relationship with the parents. After all, they say, if the family gets angry

It is very sad that it takes many children being hurt or monetary incentive for a church to move toward protecting children in their congregations.

and leaves the church, then how can they continue to help the family? My response is this: Do you really think you're helping the family when you're allowing children to be hurt?

A strong concern expressed by both service providers and, surprisingly, by pastors is that many churches are in denial that child abuse and neglect exists—especially refusal to consider that child abuse or neglect may be present within their own congregation. Unfortunately, no church or community is immune from child abuse and neglect; it may be present in varying proportions, but none are immune.

The church that refuses to acknowledge the reality of child abuse and neglect is the church that places children at risk and one that is likely harboring offenders. A church that turns a blind eye toward child abuse leaves itself wide open and its children vulnerable. A sexual offender seeks out just such a place— a place where he can have easy access to children and not be held to rules or regulations.

I must pause here to acknowledge the varying experiences of churches. Some neighborhood-based churches, particularly those in urban centers or in areas of poverty, are the first to admit that many of their members are dealing with all types of family violence. Denial is not a problem, but rather the challenge of locating resources to adequately meet the need. This challenge can be eased by collaborating with other faith communities or helping families connect with existing services in the community.

What many church leaders struggle with is the difficulty of holding families accountable and having the authority to demand change. Offenders of child abuse are not easy to confront, nor do they readily admit their wrongs. More typically, offenders will deny any wrongdoing, even in the face of overwhelming evidence. If offenders do admit to wrongdoing, they are likely to seek forgiveness quickly and make promises to never do it again. As we know, however, behaviors do not change easily or quickly.

Offenders may sound sincere, but unless true change has occurred and the hard work of rehabilitation has been accomplished, the offenses will continue and children will continue to be hurt. The church is not adequately equipped to hold offenders accountable. Often it takes a court mandate for offenders to receive the professional help they need to truly make a change.

Failure to report suspected child abuse to CPS or the police not only leaves children vulnerable to being abused, but it also breaks the law, leaving the church open to civil liability.

Many churches we spoke with believed that with God's help and power they could bring a family to health and wholeness without professional assistance. This is like saying they can heal someone of heart disease and do not need to seek a doctor's care or medication.

Yes, God is all-powerful. God also gave us humans the skills and knowledge to treat all semblances of ailments, physical and emotional. By not partnering with community professionals, a church is not allowing God to work. Just as medical doctors make mistakes, so do other professionals in the community. But that cannot stop us from going to them for help. Together, the church and the community must seek God's guidance in bringing restoration to our families and protection to our children.

Denominational responses to child safety

My students and I spoke with churches of many denominations: churches large, medium, and small in size as well as churches in urban, suburban, and rural areas. We were not able to identify any type of church that is more or less likely to be protective; there were good and bad examples in each of those categories.

One clear positive pattern that came through was the importance of the denomination in providing training materials and policies and procedures. For example, the Archdiocese of Omaha provides many training opportunities, including a curriculum called *Circle of Grace* to teach children about child abuse and neglect. All parishes affiliated with this diocese that we spoke with appeared to be protective of children.

The Catholic Church, with the immense negative fallout of sexual abuse cases, seems to be far ahead of most Protestant churches. While many Catholic churches have received the training and followed the procedures only because it was required of them, they still seem to be better prepared than most other non-Catholic churches we interviewed.

According to *Christianity Today,* an average of twenty-three new articles each day in the last three years have appeared in secular media sources revealing sexual abuse allegations arising in Protestant churches in the United States. Love and Norris (2008) state:

> Protestant denominations have been tempted to call sexual abuse a "Catholic problem"; this is simply not true. Within the past eight years, verdicts, judgments, or settlements exceeding hundreds of millions of dollars have been levied against Protestant churches for sexual abuse allegations arising from children participating in ministry programs.[1]

Many faith traditions and Christian denominations have passed resolutions or statements supporting the importance of child safety and prevention of sexual abuse. Many also provide training, consulting, and sample policies. (See appendix 3.)

The United Methodist Church, for example, has designed the Safe Sanctuaries program. Using the guidebook *Safe Sanctuaries for Children and Youth: Reducing the Risk of Abuse in the Church*,[2] area districts and local church programs seek to be welcoming and safe for children. The book, *Safe Sanctuaries for Ministers,* also provides helpful resources for churches in assessing risks and implementing processes to reduce the likelihood of abuse in congregational settings.[3] The United Methodist Church also lays out a comprehensive plan that includes issues of screening, supervision, reporting procedures, and a response plan.[4]

Another good example is the Christian Reformed Church, which established an Office of Abuse Prevention, now called Safe Church Ministry to build awareness, prevent abuse, and respond justly and effectively.[5]

The Mennonite Church is beginning to take steps toward ensuring that congregations keep children safe. Mennonite Church Canada urges its congregations to "make the Church a safe place; to prevent and minimize the possibility of the occurrence of abuse; and to protect workers from false allegations of abuse."[6] The denomination reminds its congregations that insurance companies and legal courts may consider the lack of child protection policies as a sign of negligent behavior, thereby threatening liability insurance. The "Volunteer Screening Policy and Procedures Manual" of Mennonite Church Canada states: "Any staff person or volunteer with power or authority over children or youth will be subject to the screening assessment and procedures."[7]

Mennonite Church USA passed resolutions in 1992 and 1997 denouncing the tragedy of child abuse and committing "ourselves, our congregations, and our church agencies to be communities of nonviolence, demonstrating and proclaiming the peaceful life to which Jesus Christ calls us."[8] Within the denomination, Western District Conference of Mennonite Church USA promotes Safe Sanctuaries and has developed child protection policies for all conference-sponsored events that involve children and youth and also for its year-round camping program.[9] Another helpful resource is "One Childhood Consulting," located within Franconia Mennonite Conference, which offers innovative resources and training to faith communities on child sexual abuse.[10]

The Dove's Nest Collaborative: Mennonites Keeping Children Safe, a new organization, provides sample child protection policies and training and worship resources for Mennonite Church USA congregations.[11]

Mennonite Central Committee, a worldwide ministry of Anabaptist churches including both Mennonite Church USA and Canada, also provides resources about the prevention of all types of family violence.[12]

A survey of Mennonite Church USA

Members of The Dove's Nest Collaborative recently surveyed Mennonite Church USA congregations to determine current child protection practices. Of the 850 congregations in the denomination, 269 congregations responded to the survey (32 percent) with at least one response from each of the twenty-one area conferences. Of the congregations responding, half indicated that they had a written child protection policy (52 percent). Less than half of congregations indicated that they had a written plan if they suspected a child was being abused or neglected (44 percent), and less than one-fourth indicated that they had a written plan for protecting children while also including someone with a known history of sexual offense (22 percent).

It appears that having written child safety policies in Mennonite Church USA congregations is not yet widespread. At the same time, 9 percent of respondents had suspected the abuse or neglect of a child connected to their church.

On the whole, Mennonite Church USA congregations are not yet in the practice of systematically conducting criminal background or child abuse checks on staff or volunteers. When hiring a paid staff member such as a pastor, just over half of respondents indicated that they conduct a criminal background check (57 percent), and less than half conduct a child abuse check (45 percent). In contrast, when accepting a volunteer to teach or care for children or youth, less than one-third indicated that they conduct a criminal background check (32 percent), and one-fourth conduct a child abuse check (27 percent).

The survey invited congregations to identify three things that would be the most helpful in protecting children and strengthening families. Over half of respondents asked for sample child protection policies (55 percent) and parenting resources (54 percent). Those responding also indicated they would appreciate denominational guidelines, an adult curriculum, and more information on child protection. (Full survey results available at www.DovesNest.net.)

The Christian Reformed Church conducted a similar survey in February 2010 and found that less than half of the 1,022 churches in the denomination have a child safety policy. In the survey, pastors reported wanting to learn about appropriate boundaries between church workers and youth (75 percent), to know how to report an allegation of abuse (62 percent), and to learn how to screen church workers and staff (61 percent).[13]

Vast array of services

Churches are unique in that they have the ability to have something for all members of the family, from the youngest to the oldest. Wanna-be aunties and grandparents dote on each new baby while the baby's parents beam with pride. Adoring teens hold the hands of toddlers as they move about the fellowship hall while the child's parents enjoy a break from the constant demands of parenting a toddler. Sunday school classes and playgrounds are provided for school-age children as they form lifelong friendships. Bible studies, service projects, and other gatherings engage youth. For the college age, young adults, mothers, fathers, families, and older adults, activities are available in a vast array of groupings and purposes. I cannot think of any organization outside the church that offers such a wide array of programs and services, and for free!

In a similar vein, I cannot think of any other organization where the whole family can participate together. Services and opportunities for interaction are not only welcoming and appealing to families, but the envy of any community organization. Many mental health providers desire the church's ability to have ongoing contact with families. Community counselors often struggle to get a family to come in for six sessions. The church, meanwhile, sees the family once or twice a week, year after year.

Churches are unique in that they have the ability to have something for all members of the family.

Another strength of the church lies within its own congregation: the availability of people with diverse skills and knowledge. Depending on the context of your particular faith community, your church may have teachers, social workers, medical professionals, counselors, and the list goes on. While perhaps not able to provide their expertise in an official manner, these professionals can listen and guide in ways that can be of great assistance to faith community leaders and families alike.

Jim and Andrea are long-time members of their church. They are the loving parents of two school-age children. Andrea began to experience headaches, and as the weeks passed, her headaches grew worse and she began to experience dizziness, ringing in her ears, and nausea. Before long, Andrea was confined to bed and Jim had to put in long days, filling the role of both mom and dad while continuing to hold down a full-time job.

The church played a vital role in supporting the family during this difficult time. They brought over meals, took the children on outings, and expressed their love and care through frequent visits, phone calls, cards, and assurance of constant prayer. In addition, individuals within the congregation provided assistance in their own areas of expertise. Medical professionals within the church explained the doctor's instructions. An after-school provider found two spots in her program so the kids could have a fun and safe place to be after school. A staff member in a hearing clinic offered referrals for Andrea when her hearing did not quickly return following treatment.

Jim and Andrea received support from their church in many ways and were able to return to a normal routine after several months. Even with all this help, the family endured a lot of change and stress. If this family had been without the support of their church, their extended family and neighbors may or may not have been able to provide it. It is in times like this that a family without support may slip into abuse or neglect, especially if the stressors were to stretch from months to years.

Together, the church and the community must seek God's guidance in bringing restoration to our families and protection to our children.

Depending on their educational preparation, pastors can provide short-term counseling to families in crisis. They can offer referrals for counseling and for other types of services. Larger churches are able to refer families to their own counselors on staff while smaller churches can make these referrals to community faith-based or secular agencies.

Education and training

One critical step for any faith community is educating its members about child abuse and neglect. We cannot rely on families or schools or any other entity to do this for us. Children need to know that God cares about all areas of their lives. If we expect members of our faith community to seek and receive help within the church, then we must give them the opportunity to talk about difficult things at church.

Taboo subjects, such as child abuse, sex, money, and politics

Ending Child Abuse and Neglect in our Churches / 147

cannot be checked at the door of the church but welcomed in and discussed in our classes, small groups, and from our pulpits. Where do you want the children in your community to learn about the hard things of life and gain their values?

Also our churches need to teach a theology of love and value for children and to encourage and model positive discipline. Parent-child relationships should not be punitive but mutually respectful and life-giving. Using images in the Bible of God as our loving parent, we can promote healthy relationships in our families.

When a faith community's members have more knowledge of child abuse and neglect, they are better equipped to respond and help families.

In our churches, adults—especially teachers, youth leaders, and caretakers—need education on how to protect children and strengthen families, how to identify abuse and neglect, and how to respond when abuse and neglect are suspected. When a faith community's members have more knowledge of child abuse and neglect (prevalence, signs of abuse, risk factors), they are better equipped to respond and help families. Through education, churches can break out of denial, protect their children, and offer more assistance to at risk families. When church members know more about child abuse and neglect, they will understand the complexity of the issue and be less judgmental and less likely to try to handle it on their own.

Many types of child abuse and neglect exist, and we need to be equipped to identify and respond to any of them. While many churches are primarily concerned about sexual abuse, and they should be concerned, other types of abuse and neglect are more prevalent in the communities in which we live and work. As faith communities, we need to be aware of all types of abuse and neglect, and be poised to protect children in all places that we encounter them.

Making referrals

 Churches can play a significant role in connecting families and children with needed resources. Through their emphasis on relationships, their ongoing contact with families, and their many programs, churches have the opportunity to identify kids and families at risk. Churches can then connect families with counseling, job training, housing, food pantries, and parenting classes, and keep families from sinking further into the quagmire that may lead to abuse. If a child is already being hurt, the church can make the report to the authorities, and thereby participate in providing safety for that child and connecting the family with the help they need.

While most church leaders are eager to make referrals to community agencies, it is sometimes frustrating to know where to refer families. We don't usually want to make a referral unless we know to whom we are sending them. Particularly for counseling referrals, most churches want to refer families only to faith-based counseling agencies. Do not automatically refrain from referring a family to a non-faith-based counseling agency. Many secular counseling agencies have Christian counselors on staff; even if they do not, most professionally trained counselors will respect a client's spiritual perspective and use it as a framework for healing.

Some churches work proactively to form partnerships with community counseling agencies. For example, they designate funds out of their budget to support a local counseling agency, and in turn, this agency provides services to people from that church at a lower cost. Along with this partnership comes a relationship that seems to enhance the meeting of everyone's needs, especially the families who are in need of the services.

Another critical step in effectively referring a child or family for help is to know the program's contact information, hours of operation, and eligibility criteria. It's not as easy as you may think for a family to get food from a food pantry.

For example, the family has to live in the right geographical area, have the required identification, be available during the hours of operation, and be able to get to the food pantry and transport the food home. In addition, the parents may not be able or want to take the children with them, so they'll need to find childcare. Perhaps the family doesn't speak or write English, but the program's staff people speak only English, or their forms are only in English. Perhaps the family has received help from the food pantry a couple of months ago and needs to wait a few more months before being eligible again. And last, but certainly not least, perhaps the family is ashamed to ask for help or does not know how to ask for help.

It's a great idea to accompany a family when helping them to receive needed services. Consider going with the parent to the food pantry or the welfare office. Not only can you help the parent overcome barriers like communication or paperwork or transportation, but you can also model help-seeking behavior and you can learn a lot about the agency.

Those of us who have never had to ask for help really have no idea how hard it is to access help. The best thing we can do is become familiar with all the possible barriers to a family's accessing of services, and do all we can to help them overcome these barriers.

Consider the list of "Ten great things a church can do for families." Like Jesus, may we desire to "gather [the] children together as a hen protects her chicks beneath her wings" (Luke 13:34). What can you do today?

Ten Great Things a Church Can Do for Families

1. Offer activities and services for people of all ages.

2. Support families—offer assistance with babysitting, transportation, homework, or home repair.

3. Educate adults in your church on child abuse and neglect, healthy parenting, and safety.

4. Educate children and youth in your church on child abuse and neglect, and safety (age appropriate).

5. Pray for children and families in your community.

6. Be prepared to provide referrals to families for food, clothing, shelter, counseling, and more.

7. Make new friends in your community—take cookies to neighbors, interact with children in your neighborhood, swap resources, car pool.

8. Start a clothes closet or food pantry, or contribute to an established one.

9. Volunteer in a community agency—sort donations, answer the phone, help with mailings or a fundraiser, or visit families.

10. Report suspected child abuse and neglect to CPS or the police.

Discussion Questions

1. What are some areas that you think your church could improve in protecting children? In strengthening families?
2. What are ways that the church has been supportive of you and your family during a difficult time? How did this feel?
3. What do you think about this statement: "The church that refuses to acknowledge the reality of child abuse and neglect

is the church that places children at risk and a church that is likely harboring offenders."

4. Where would you refer a parent for:
    - counseling?
    - help with parenting?
    - help with housing?
    - getting a job?
    - getting food for their family?

How many of these places have you visited yourself?

Action Items

1. Find scriptures in the Bible that tell of God as a loving parent.
2. Find a curriculum to teach your children about safety. Talk with the children's education director at your church about what you found.
3. Invite a class or small group in your church to study this book. Perhaps you could teach it.
4. Review the programs of your church. Is there an age group that may need more services or activities? Talk with your church leadership about this need. Better yet, volunteer to do something about it.
5. How many of the "Ten great things" is your church doing? What is one more thing you could be doing?

Chapter 12

Child Abuse Prevention Policies in our Churches

O people, the LORD has told you what is good, and this is what he requires of you: to do what is right, to love mercy, and to walk humbly with your God.

—Micah 6:8

Every church needs a written child abuse prevention policy. Our children are too important, too precious to leave their safety to chance. Having a child abuse prevention policy will help to keep your children safe, and it will communicate to families within your church that the safety of their children is a high priority.

This chapter outlines the elements to include in a child abuse prevention policy; a sample policy is provided in appendix 4. Most elements of this chapter pertain to preventing the sexual abuse of children. This is the type of abuse that is most at risk within the church setting.

A child abuse prevention policy must be carefully constructed to cover several important areas, and it is best when tailored to your unique congregation. It is important to include many parties when writing and seeking approval for a child abuse prevention policy; parents, children's teachers, and youth leaders come to mind first. Others to include are anyone on staff, including pastors, and those responsible for facilities.

A child abuse prevention policy must be made visible and available to all, members and visitors alike. You may want to post it on your website and put it up on bulletin boards. Making the policy public will help to deter any sex offenders looking for a church that is an easy mark.

Every church needs to have a written child abuse prevention policy. Our children are too important, too precious to leave their safety to chance.

Once a year, distribute copies to your staff, Sunday school teachers, youth ministers, and anyone who works regularly with children. Better yet, ask them to sign a form acknowledging that they have read and understood the policy.

A particularly important point: Child abuse does not occur within church facilities or during formal church programs as often as it does in someone's home, in a car, or in a park during informal get-togethers. A sexual offender will typically use church activities to build rapport with the child and the family but then lure the child into other settings to commit the actual abuse. This is why it is absolutely important that prevention policies cover informal gatherings as much as they do formal gatherings. Be especially mindful of overnight youth activities, camps, and retreats, including those sponsored by or with other organizations.

Once you have a written child abuse prevention policy, it is of vital importance that you implement the policy. A big step is to appoint individuals to be responsible for implementing the policy. Depending on the extent of changes needed, a budget may be required.

Education and training for teachers, leaders, and parents

Child abuse and neglect is multi-dimensional; training must be as well. One year you may want to teach the specifics of child abuse and neglect. The next year you may want to focus on topics such as child development, healthy relationships, first aid, dating violence, or any of the protective and risk factors discussed in an earlier chapter.

At a minimum, provide training for those who teach or care for children and youth. Since nearly all adults have contact with children in some capacity—as a grandparent or neighbor, or seeing children at a grocery store, park, or restaurant—all adults should be trained to recognize child abuse and neglect and to know what they can do.

Strive to provide training in various ways and places. For example, a sermon could be given on healthy family relationships or on protecting those who are most vulnerable. Include in the service related poems, prayers, and responsive readings (see appendix 6 and additional worship resources at www.DovesNest. net). Training can be just as effective when it is less formal as in a Sunday school class, small group, or retreat setting.

Be creative in how you provide training for adults and children on child abuse and neglect prevention. Give participants plenty of opportunity to engage in discussions and role-plays. Discuss scenarios in this book or from the local news. This is a tough topic. Unless we give our class participants the opportunity to grapple with this, they may not remember much and their attitudes and behaviors are unlikely to budge.

No matter the context for providing training on child abuse, always assume that someone in the audience has experienced abuse, and if not someone in the audience then someone an audience member cares about. You may be surprised to know how many people around you are survivors of abuse. Be sensitive to their experiences and to the emotions such training may bring out in them. They may withdraw, cry, become angry, or want to be very actively involved in discussion.

Survivors of child abuse may or may not want to talk about their experiences—this needs to be left up to them. If someone does want to share a personal story of abuse, be sure to provide this individual with safety and support. Allowing her to practice and to prepare for her own emotions and the possible emotional reactions of others is important. If someone spontaneously shares her own story or pieces of it during a class or small group, leaders must be prepared to respond in a way that is helpful to both the individual and the group.

When responding to someone who becomes angry over a particular topic or method of delivering material, remember that this individual may have personal experiences of abuse which may be triggering this response. Listen attentively to what people are saying, ask open-ended questions, and pay attention to nonverbal behaviors. Having a list of referrals for professional assistance is particularly helpful for these situations. (See appendixes 5 and 6.)

Education and training for children and youth

While not responsible for protecting themselves, children do need education on how to be safe. Trainings must be offered frequently, from different perspectives, and in a manner appropriate to the age and developmental level of children participating.

When providing education and training on child abuse and neglect to children, we must be very careful to present information in such a way that children can understand and will not be unduly frightened. As we know, children are not simply small adults. Children receive, understand, and filter information in ways that are unique to their level of development.

I spoke with a child who had just participated in a sexual abuse prevention program at school. When asked what she learned, she said, "When someone touches you in bad ways, you should jump out the window." While I seriously doubt this was the intended message, this is the one received by the child.

Some tactics may cause a child to become wary of all adults, including family members, friends, and strangers. Children and youth need healthy relationships with adults, and they need to not be afraid to pursue these relationships and explore life in healthy ways. We need to help our children identify safe people in their lives and foster open relationships with these people. They must be encouraged to speak with a trusted adult when they have questions or something feels uncomfortable to them.

Before providing education to children or youth, inform and include their parents. Parents need to be informed of the material that will be presented to their children so they can be prepared to rein-force the message and help the children apply it to the multiple settings in which their children find themselves, such as home, church, school, neighborhood, and family get-togethers.

Education must be provided in a way and at a level that can be understood and accepted by its students.

It is critical to give parents the opportunity to participate in the selection of topics, materials, and exercises to be used with their children. It is also a good idea to welcome parents to the classes with their children so they may also learn the techniques and language learned by the children. Even if the parents do not take you up on the invitation, you will secure their support.

If a parent does not participate or allow the child to partici-pate, make the education and materials available to the family in another way. We cannot force this information onto anyone, but we can do all we can to make it available.

As a result of providing information about child abuse, a child or youth may make an outcry or want to speak with someone about something that concerns him or doesn't seem right. Be sure teachers are prepared to listen and respond to children; put procedures in place for reporting to the authori-ties and making referrals.

Research studies show that many child abuse prevention programs aimed at children do not produce the intended results. Sometimes children do not understand the material; quite often children do not retain the material or they are unduly fright-ened by it. One example of a promising curriculum is *Circle of Grace*.[1] In this program, children are taught they were created by God and are special. They learn about the "circle of grace" that can help them to be safe in a large variety of settings. Many other books, videos, and curriculum on the topic can be considered. A list of children's books is included in appendix 7.

Since abuse and neglect can occur in so many contexts and in so many ways, it is doubtful that children would be able to apply what they've learned and keep themselves safe. As adults, we must bear the responsibility for keeping children safe.

Child abuse and neglect response plan

We hope the day does not come that we suspect a child within our church has been abused or neglected, but we need to have a plan in case it does. Include in your church's written child abuse prevention policy who will make the report to CPS or the police, when this will be done, and how this will be documented. See the "Frequently Asked Questions on Reporting Child Abuse or Neglect" in appendix 2.

Usually, it is advisable that the individual to whom the child made the outcry or who witnessed the abuse make the report; this report should be made as promptly as possible. Quite likely, the individual will want help and support in making the report.

Work cooperatively and openly with the authorities, and ask how you can be supportive to the investigation while also supporting the child and family. Make a plan for notifying church leadership and parents about the abuse allegations and subsequent report to CPS or the police. Consider how you will handle the individual against whom the allegations have been made until the case has been closed or the situation resolved.

Anyone who has dealt with abuse and neglect knows that each situation is unique and each situation requires our full attention and an array of knowledge and skills. A situation of abuse never appears at a convenient time and is never straightforward. It is always gut-wrenching.

Many pastors expressed to us how very difficult it is to deal with abuse allegations, regardless of their relationship with the alleged victim and alleged offender, and non-offending family members. We go through intense agony as we struggle with whether or not to report, how to keep the child safe, what to say to the child's parent(s), and what to say to other parents and individuals in our church community.

Because of the importance of confidentiality, church leaders may feel unable to process these difficult decisions with others, and feel the weight of the responsibility on their own shoulders. Some pastors expressed how they have felt alienated by members of their church when making a report of abuse or when reaching out to an alleged offender.

These situations are complex, difficult, and multifaceted. One role that denominations or interchurch alliances may take is to support pastors and others who find themselves dealing with the vast and overwhelming challenges of working with families and keeping children safe. Having clear policies and procedures in place is a tremendous asset when wading through these choppy waters. Thinking through and documenting various contingencies prior to an emergency is critical when faced with a difficult situation.

Background checks

Many churches now conduct background checks on all staff and volunteers. Although they would often prefer to rely on trust and gut instincts when selecting teachers and other leaders for children and youth ministry, most churches have come to realize the importance of the background check. Background checks can identify individuals who have been convicted of crimes or identified as a child abuse offender.

A background check needs to be conducted on all individuals who have access to children. Of course, this includes pastors, youth ministers, and Sunday school teachers, but this also includes custodians, bus drivers, and nursery workers.

Ninety-nine times out of a hundred, background checks will come back clean; however, that one time a background check does not come back clean will be proof enough for your church to continue this practice. None of us ever want to find out that if we had only taken the precaution of a background check, we would have been able to protect a child from being hurt. Even if all the background checks you run come back clean, you will never know how many child abuse offenders were deterred from victimizing children in your church because they knew they would be caught with the background check.

You'll never know how many child abuse offenders were deterred from victimizing children in your church because they knew they'd be caught with the background check.

(See "Frequently Asked Questions on Background Checks" in appendix 8.)

Remember that conducting background checks is not a sufficient child abuse prevention strategy on its own. Sadly, child sex offenders often have many victims before they are ever caught or convicted. Until convicted, they do not show up on registries for sex offenders. In addition, background checks may not extend outside your state or most certainly do not extend outside your country. While the background check is important, many additional steps must be taken in order to ensure the safety of our children.

Supervision

Adequate supervision is a critical piece of a church's safety plan. The two-adult rule is important. It means that a minimum of two adults must provide supervision for children at all times. Having two adults is helpful in many ways, but specific to child abuse, the presence of two adults greatly diminishes the opportunity for abuse and provides a witness if allegations of abuse are made. A youth worker, for example, in the nursery does not replace the need for two adults.

Of utmost importance is that a child is never alone with an adult unless in the direct view of others. This prohibits, for example, an adult from being alone in a car with a child or youth. Arrangements need to be made ahead of time to ensure adequate supervision at all times and in all settings.

Facilities

As churches, we need to take the steps necessary to ensure that our church facilities and grounds are safe for children and welcoming for all. An environmental scan of all church facilities and grounds is important to make sure that children can be kept safe. A safety checklist for the home can be adapted to the church to include covering outlets, controlling access to sharp objects (sharp scissors in Sunday school rooms, knives in the kitchen, chemicals under the sink), *Creating a safe environment is not only important for child abuse prevention, but also for welcoming families with young children.* securing loose rugs, hanging cords, and covering up sharp corners. Fully stocked first-aid kits are an important part of a safety plan.

Creating a safe environment is not only important for child abuse prevention but also for welcoming families with young children. I remember talking with the mother of a toddler at the end of a Sunday morning together in church. She was exhausted! There were simply so many dangers present in the church building that she had spent the entire morning chasing after her toddler to keep him safe. She told me that she was tempted to call it quits with the church until her child was older. We don't want this to be the experience of our families with young children. Church needs to be a safe place for all.

An important move, and one more specific to child abuse, is to provide windows in all doors, including classrooms and the pastor's office. No rooms in our churches should be completely private; windows need to allow observation of all rooms.

Another very important consideration is to require other organizations or groups that use your church facilities to follow child protection practices. Don't be like the church I saw on the TV news. The reporter was standing in front of the church sign and telling the story of a child sexual abuse investigation.

While the sexual abuse did occur in the church facilities, it did not occur in a program of the church. The church was allowing an after-school program to use its facilities. Even though the staff did not attend the church, it was the church's name that viewers saw on the 10 o'clock news. Check with your insurance provider to learn about this and other liability concerns when allowing others to use your church facilities.

Key personnel

Another important component to a church's safety procedures is to identify key personnel to monitor safety policies and be consulted if child abuse is suspected. If your church has a policy, it is very important that this policy be made public and implemented. Having a policy and not following it shows that you know better but are not willing to invest the time and energy into following it. Identify key personnel to make sure your church's child abuse policies are followed. You can do this by appointing a leadership board, perhaps using the same way other church leaders are selected.

Presence of a known sex offender

We can assume that sex offenders will visit or attend our churches—sometimes we will know they are there, and sometimes we will not. The above-stated policies will help to protect our children from unknown risks. Other times, an individual may begin to attend your church or ask to attend your church, and will be known as a previous sex offender. In our hearts, we know that churches should be open to all people, but acting on that knowledge is sometimes a struggle for us.

Safety procedures can be put in place and documented in a child abuse policy to allow a previous sex offender to attend our churches. First, the previous sex offender must be completely willing to follow guidelines set forth by the church. At a most basic level, he or she will not be allowed any unsupervised contact with children and will not be allowed any role in leading or teaching children, including teaching or helping in Sunday school, leading youth ministry, and being involved in children's music or transportation. All parents of children must be notified in a respectful manner that a previous sex offender is attending the church (or wanting to attend) and notified of the safety procedures in place. A meeting with all parents may be helpful. Your church could also designate adult-only spaces in which the offender can participate.

If a previous sex offender is truly committed to rehabilitation, he or she will follow all the rules set forth. If not, he or she can be asked to leave, for the sake of child safety.

When you encounter resistance

Incorporating safety procedures into our churches to ensure the safety of our children may require change and work. Some folks may come with the attitude: "My church didn't do this when they raised me and I turned out all right, so why is it important that we know and do all this now?" As humans, we are reluctant to face change, especially change that hints that we or someone we love may have been wrong in the past.

First, we have more information now about dangers and risks to our children than we did in the past, and we must act in accordance with this new information. Plus, our children are now at risk in new ways and in new proportions. Previous ways of parenting and keeping children safe may have been adequate then, but they may not be adequate now. In reality, we may also discover that there was a lot more abuse going on in the good old days than we realize—we just may not have called it abuse.

Even though you may feel totally comfortable with everyone in your church, what will you do when someone new shows up and asks to teach Sunday school, help with youth activities, or drive kids home from an activity? On what grounds will you allow this new person to participate? Unless you have written guidelines prepared ahead of time, it will be quite awkward to write guidelines or begin enforcing guidelines after someone who is questionable shows up and wants to participate. For the sake of our children and youth, we must anticipate these kinds of situations and be prepared.

When someone is resistant to any element of a child safety policy, sit down and talk face-to-face with that person about the concerns. The cause for a person's resistance may be any number of factors, and until we take the time to listen, we cannot find resolution. Basic education on abuse and raising awareness on the existence of the problem will help to alleviate most resistance.

Next steps

We have come so far. We now understand much more about the problem of child abuse and neglect and are thinking about our role as faith communities. Our task as faith communities to prevent and respond to the tragedy of child abuse and neglect is humongous. We must not be paralyzed by the immensity of the task but rather seek God's direction in determining next steps for us. We may not be able to save the world (at least not today), but we can certainly seek to improve our corner of it.

A great next step is to assess your current situation. Use the checklist in appendix 9 to determine what you are already doing well and what you need to improve. You can then prioritize the areas of improvement to determine what is the most important to do first.

Faith communities have an incredible capacity to positively influence the lives of children and families. While they may not be labeled "child abuse prevention activities," many of the activities in your church strengthen children and families alike. Child protection must be a comprehensive effort that is ever-evolving. Our children are much too valuable to not take their safety very seriously.

Our children are entrusted to us. They cannot defend themselves. We must do all we can to protect them now before anything ever happens. We do not want to have to say to a child that we are sorry for not protecting him or her.

Discussion Questions

1. If your church has a written child abuse prevention policy, read it over.
   - Prior to this class, did you know your church had a policy?
   - Did you know what was written in the policy?
   - What are the strengths of the policy?
   - To what extent is the policy implemented and followed?
   - What recommendations do you have for improving the policy?
2. If your church does not have a written child abuse prevention policy, discuss what would be important elements to a policy. You may want to use the sample policy in the appendix as a springboard for discussion (see appendix 4).
   - What steps would need to be taken to adopt a policy in your church?
   - What might be some of the barriers to adopting a policy in your church?
3. What concerns do you have about the safety of children in your church? Where and when are they most vulnerable?
4. Which people or groups in your church can you commend for keeping your children safe?

Action Items

1. Complete the checklist in appendix 9.
2. Take action to remedy any issues identified in the checklist.
3. Talk with other churches in your neighborhood or conference about what you have learned and done. Challenge them to take needed steps to protect the children and strengthen the families in their communities.

Appendix 1

Parenting Curricula

Updated weblinks can be found at www.DovesNest.net/LetTheChildrenCome

Systematic Training for Effective Parenting (STEP)

Websites: http://us.mcc.org/programs/women/resources/parenting
and www.steppublishers.com
Languages: English and Spanish

Through this seven-session program, parents learn how to use nonviolent, positive parenting strategies to raise confident and cooperative children. Suggestions include giving choices, active listening, and logical consequences. This series covers the topics of understanding yourself and your child, understanding beliefs and feelings, understanding children's misbehavior, encouraging your child and yourself, listening and talking to your child, helping children cooperate, discipline that makes sense, and choosing your approach to discipline. Two training systems are available: one for parents of children under age six and one for parents of children ages seven to eighteen.

Active Parenting

Website: www.activeparenting.com
Languages: English and Spanish

This program gives parents the needed skills to raise cooperative, responsible, and emotionally healthy children. Nonviolent, positive discipline techniques are taught to help parents avoid power struggles with their children. Six sessions cover topics such as parenting styles, handling problems, teaching responsibility, understanding why children misbehave, sidestepping power struggles, and building self-esteem in children. Several modules are available: early childhood, ages five to twelve, and preteens and teens. Training programs are available for divorced parents and stepfamilies.

Common Sense Parenting

Website: www.parenting.org
Languages: English and Spanish

This book was developed from the Common Sense Parenting training program at Boys Town in Omaha, Nebraska. The eighteen chapters cover such topics as positive and negative consequences, teaching self-control, and reaching goals with charts and contracts. Parents learn how to reduce their children's problem behaviors, improve family satisfaction, and build strong relationships with their children. Workbooks and supplemental CDs/DVDs are available. A training for trainers workshop is available.

Effective Black Parenting

Website: www.ciccparenting.org
Languages: English

Due to history of racism and discrimination, black families have unique needs. The Effective Black Parenting curriculum was designed to address these needs in a culturally sensitive manner. Participants learn parenting skills such as time-out and effective praise to be used with children of all socioeconomic and cultural backgrounds. In addition, parents learn culturally specific parenting strategies such as traditional black discipline vs. modern black self-discipline and pride in blackness. This program is designed to be taught in fifteen three-hour sessions.

Nurturing Parenting Program

Website: www.nurturingparenting.com
Languages: English and Spanish

The Nurturing Parenting Programs are a family-centered initiative designed to build nurturing parenting skills as an alternative to abusive and neglectful parenting and child-rearing practices. Parents and their children attend separate group sessions that aim to increase empathy, encourage appropriate behaviors, build self-esteem, and help the family learn to have fun together. After meeting separately for two hours, parents and children come together to sing songs, play games, and have fun as a family. Parents of children ages birth to five attend twenty-seven weekly sessions. Those with children ages five to eleven attend fifteen weekly sessions. Parents of children ages twelve to eighteen attend twelve weekly sessions. There is also a training program of twenty-six sessions for teen parents.

Parenting with Love and Logic (Becoming a Love and Logic Parent)

Website: www.loveandlogic.com
Languages: English and Spanish

Love and Logic provides parents with simple and easy-to-use child-rearing techniques that create less stress and more fun for the family. This twelve- to fifteen-hour training program aims to help parents raise responsible children, easily change their children's behavior, and have more fun as parents. Topics covered include distinguishing between parenting styles, avoiding power struggles, teaching responsibility to children, and setting limits. A separate training for parents of children ages birth to six is also available.

Appendix 2

Frequently Asked Questions on Reporting Child Abuse or Neglect

1. What if I'm not sure?

- Think about the facts—what did the child tell you? What did you observe? What did you hear? Don't second-guess the facts. Report what you heard and saw.
- Talk with someone who is knowledgeable about child abuse and neglect and/or the family (but don't let this delay you too long in making the report).
- Think about the abuse from the perspective of the child(ren), not the possible abuser. Is the child safe? Does the child need protecting?
- Think about how you would feel if the child is hurt and you hadn't done anything.
- If you decide not to report, write down what you observed and heard along with the date and save for future reference.

2. Whom should I call?

In the United States call either Child Protective Services (CPS) or your local police (911). Most U.S. states have a toll-free child

172 / Appendix 2

abuse hotline—look in a phone book or on the internet. In the United States, you could also call the National Child Abuse Hotline at 1-800-4ACHILD (1-800-422-4453) and they will direct you.

In Canada call either your local children's aid society, your province's social service ministry, or your local police.

3. Will I have to give my name?

Including your name and contact information when you report abuse is not required, but encouraged. The authorities may want to seek more information from you; when possible, they may share the outcome of their investigation with you. If the alleged abuse is found to be untrue by the authorities, the case will be closed and you as the reporter will not be held liable, as you were reporting in good faith. By law, CPS or the police cannot give your name to the family—this would only come up if the case were to go to court.

4. What will child protection authorities do?

In the United States CPS will first assign a level of urgency to your report based on the safety of the child. If the child's safety is at immediate risk, particularly if the child is very young, CPS and local police may seek to locate the child immediately. If the child's safety is deemed to be at high to moderate risk, CPS may locate the child within two to fourteen days of your report. CPS may deem that the information is inadequate at this time and close the case without contacting the child or family. (Time frames vary by state or province.) If adequate information supporting abuse or neglect is given in your report, the authorities will investigate or assess the case by interviewing the child, then the siblings and parent(s), the alleged offender, and other parties, if needed. In this assessment, the authorities will gather evidence to determine the safety of the child and determine the likelihood that child abuse or neglect occurred, based on your state or province's definitions of child abuse and neglect. This stage may take two to six weeks.

Depending on the outcome of the assessment and available resources, child protection authorities will provide direct services or referrals to keep the child safe and strengthen the family. Sometimes a report to the authorities can be very helpful to families in accessing services that may not have been available without your report. (Procedures in your state, province, or territory may vary somewhat from those described above.)

5. How quickly will the child be removed from the home?

The goal of the authorities is not to remove children from families; the goal of authorities is to keep children safe. If it is deemed that a child's safety is at very high risk, the authorities will work in conjunction with the police to remove a child from the home. In the United States a child can be removed from the home for only 48 hours before a judge must hear the case at an emergency hearing and determine if the child can be returned to the home or needs to remain in out-of-home care. (Time frames may vary by state or province.)

6. What do I tell the child or parent?

What you tell the child or parent(s) depends on many factors: your relationship with the child and family, the child's age, and the nature of the alleged abuse or neglect. You may want to tell the child and/or family that you are concerned about the child's safety and remind them of the responsibility to report child abuse and neglect. If a parent is not responsible for the alleged abuse, you can encourage the parent to make the report to CPS, therefore giving the parent the opportunity to be protective (you may want to make your own report as well). Telling the parents that you are making a report to CPS may be risky, especially if one parent is the alleged offender; this may put the child at greater risk or the family may disappear. When you make a report to CPS, let them know what you have told the parents and ask what you should do or not do in regards to the child and family.

7. I'm feeling sad/confused/angry about reporting abuse—is this normal?

Absolutely. Reporting child abuse or neglect feels awful. On one hand, you feel frightened for the child, but on the other hand, you wonder if you're making too big a deal of what you saw or observed. Perhaps you doubt your own eyes or ears. It doesn't help that it may feel like you're tattling on someone. You may also feel angry toward the alleged abuser.

Here are some tips on what you can do:
- Focus on the child's need for safety and remind yourself that you acted on the information you had available to you at that time.
- Remember that no child deserves to be hurt or placed in harm's way.
- Seek the support of someone who is knowledgeable of child abuse and neglect and talk about your feelings (but remember to protect the confidentiality of the child and/or family).
- Write your thoughts and feelings in a journal.
- Hug your own family members.
- Do something that you find comforting: talk to a friend, exercise, listen to music, read a book.
- Immerse yourself in your regular daily activities.

8. I've reported, now what do I do?

As much as possible, resume your normal relationship with the child and/or family. Provide immediate assistance if that seems appropriate and possible. Continue to ensure the safety of the child and other children, to offer assistance to the family, and report further concerns, if needed.

9. What if the child protection authorities don't do anything?

The authorities may not respond as quickly as you wish or in the way that you wish. They must work within the constraints of their context and must find evidence of abuse or neglect in order to take action. You can report suspected abuse and neglect again later, and this time, more evidence may be available. In the meantime, remain available to the child and parents, as appropriate.

10. If the child is removed, can I care for the child?

It is quite normal for you to want to take the child into your arms and into your home and protect him or her from any further danger. If the child cannot remain at home, the authorities will determine the best placement for the child. With the safety of the child at the center of their considerations, the authorities may place the child with a family member or family friend, in a foster home, or in a group home. You can let the authorities know of your desire to care for the child.

Denominational Statements and Resources on Child/ Sexual Abuse

Explore this non-exhaustive list of websites related to child abuse, sexual abuse, and other forms of family violence from various denominations. Also included are websites related to child/sexual abuse from three insurance companies that provide coverage to churches. Updated website links can be found at www.DovesNest.net/LetTheChildrenCome.

American Baptist Church
Resolution Against Sexual Exploitation of Children: www.abc-usa.org/Resources/ABCResources/PolicyStatementsResoultions/tabid/199/Default.aspx

The Anglican Church of Canada
Sexual Misconduct Policy Applicable to National Staff and Volunteers: www.anglican.ca/about/departments/gso/documents/Sexual-Misconduct-Policy.pdf

Canadian Conference of Catholic Bishops
From Pain to Hope: www.cccb.ca/site/Files/From_Pain_To_Hope.pdf and www.cccb.ca/site/Files/TaskForceGroup_A.pdf

Christian Church (Disciples of Christ)
The Church Takes Steps to Prevent Abuse:
www.discipleshomemissions.org/files/FCM-ChildAbuse.pdf
Discipline and the Church's Ministry with Children:
www.discipleshomemissions.org/files/FCM-Disciplinefor
Children.pdf

Christian Reformed Church in North America
Safe Church Ministry: www.crcna.org/safechurch

Church of the Brethren
Child Protection: www.brethren.org/site/PageServer?
pagename=grow_family_ministries_child_protection

Church of the Nazarene
Child Safety Protection Guidelines: www.nazarene.org/
ministries/ssm/children/resources/safety/guidelines/display.
aspx

The Episcopal Church
Model Policies for the Protection of Children and Youth from
Abuse: http://download.cpg.org/insurance/publications/pdf/
larg_font_model_policies.pdf

Evangelical Lutheran Church of America
An ELCA Strategy for Responding to Sexual Abuse in the Church:
www.elca.org/Growing-In-Faith/Vocation/Rostered-Leadership/
Leadership-Support/Safe-Place/General-Resources.aspx
Called to be a Safe Place: www2.elca.org/safeplace/

Friends General Conference (Quaker)
Policy on Abuse Prevention: www.fgcquaker.org/connect/
summer05/child_abuse_policy.htm

The Lutheran Church, Missouri Synod
Child Abuse: www.lcms.org/pages/internal.asp?NavID=15823

Mennonite Brethren (Canadian Conference)
Executive Board Clarifies Position on Sexual Abuse: www.mbconf. ca/home/products_and_services/resources/publications/mb_herald/ mb_herald_april_2009/people_and_events/homepage

Mennonite Church Canada
Volunteer Screening for a Safe Church: www.mennonitechurch. ca/resourcecentre/ResourceView/5/10027
Volunteer Screening Policy and Procedures Manual: www.mennonitechurch.ca/resourcecentre/ResourceView/5/10018

Mennonite Church USA
And No One Shall Make Them Afraid (1997): www.mcusa-archives.org/library/resolutions/nooneshallmakethemafraid.html
Resolution Against Interpersonal Abuse (1992): www.gameo. org/encyclopedia/contents/R484.html#A Resolution against Interpersonal Abuse
Resolution on Male Violence Against Women (1993): www.gameo. org/encyclopedia/contents/R48647.html
Denominational Ministry Packet on Sexual Misconduct (2000): www.mennoniteusa.org/Default.aspx?tabid=241

Presbyterian Church USA
Creating Safe Churches–Addressing Sexual Misconduct www.pcusa. org/sexualmisconduct/index.htm
We Won't Let It Happen Here! Preventing Child Abuse in the Church: http://safety.synodsun.com/images/PCUSA-policyguide.pdf

Southern Baptist Convention
On Protecting Children from Abuse: www.sbc.net/resolutions/ amResolution.asp?ID=1173

The United Church of Canada
Sexual Abuse Policy and Procedures: www.united-church.ca/
files/handbooks/sexualabuse.pdf

Unitarian Universalist

Balancing Acts–Keeping Children Safe in Congregations: www.uua.
org/leaders/safecongregations/balancingacts/index.shtml

United Church of Christ

Safety and Protection of Children in Church: www.ucc.org/
justice/children-and-youth/safety-and-protection-of.html

United Methodist Church

www.gcfa.org/sexualGenderHMP.html
Safe Sanctuaries–Protecting Our Children and Youth: www.
safesanctuaries.org/conference_policy/index.html
Violence Against Women and Children: http://archives.umc.org/
interior.asp?ptid=4&mid=6732

United States Conference of Catholic Bishops

Charter for the Protection of Children and Young People:
www.usccb.org/ocyp/charter.shtml

Insurance Groups

Brotherhood Mutual: www.brotherhoodmutual.com/safetycentral/
articles/navart26.htm
Church Mutual: www.churchmutual.com/index.php/choice/
risk/page/Ads_abuse/id/35_
Guide One: www.guideone.com/safetyresources/churches/
youthindex.htm

Appendix 4

Sample Child Protection and Abuse Response Policy _____(name of church)

Introduction

Each child is a special gift from God. We acknowledge the high value that Jesus placed on children during his earthly ministry. We seek to make all our church activities and facilities safe, especially for children. It is our responsibility as adults to do all we can to protect children.

Sadly, child abuse is prevalent. It is hurting children, families, and societies everywhere. According to Nebraska Health and Human Services (*replace with your state's or province's laws*):

> There are three definitions used to describe abuse:
> 1. *Physical abuse* exists when a child has a non-accidental injury.
> 2. *Emotional abuse* exists when parents always put blame on a child or always reject the child.
> 3. *Sexual abuse* exists when an adult uses a child as a part of any type of sexual act.
>
> *Neglect* is defined in two ways. *Emotional neglect* is when the child suffers from a parent not giving chances for feeling loved, wanted, secure,

and worthy. *Physical neglect* is when a parent does not provide basic needs or a safe place to live. Examples are: not having enough food or clothing; not following doctor's orders; not providing the supervision needed to keep the child safe; or not having heat in the winter.[1]

Child abuse prevention within our church community

We must be prepared in both knowledge and practice to prevent all types of child abuse and neglect and to strengthen families. This policy applies to all church ministries, including but not limited to Sunday school, youth activities, vacation Bible school, mentoring, and nursery. We commit to:

1. Offer trainings.
   a. Annually, training and materials will be offered to all adults in the congregation and especially to teachers and leaders of children. Training may be specific to child abuse or may be on a related topic such as child safety, child development, healthy family relationshiops, or any protective or risk factor for abuse.
   b. Every two years for all children (ages six to eighteen) related to child abuse and/or child safety (such as safe touch for elementary-aged children or dating violence for adolescents). This training should be appropriate to the child's age group. Parents must be included in the selection of material and involved in the screening of any books, movies, or other materials. Parents will be invited to participate in training with their child(ren).

2. Make our church facility safe for children.
   a. Place windows in all doors where children or youth ministry is conducted (Sunday school rooms, pastor's office).

   b. A fully stocked first-aid kit will be available in the church building.

3. Provide safe and adequate supervision to children.

   a. Follow a *two-adult rule*, especially at overnight activities involving children and when activities are being conducted in homes or other private locations.

   b. A youth (eighteen years or younger) should never teach/care for children alone without a supervising adult available.

   c. A parent must always be notified ahead of time and give consent for his or her child to be transported away from church facilities.

   d. No physical discipline (hitting, slapping) may be used. When a child misbehaves, an adult may use redirection and/or verbal means to guide the child's behavior. If this does not work, the child shall be taken to his or her parent for further action.

4. Attend to related personnel issues.

   a. Annually each teacher and leader of children will be presented a copy of the congregation's child protection and abuse response policy and asked to acknowledge that he or she has read and will abide by the policy.

   b. A background check, including child abuse and sex offender registries and criminal history will be conducted on final candidates for all church staff positions, including the pastor and custodians, before hiring. A background check will also be run on all Sunday school teachers, youth leaders, and nursery workers. These background checks must be conducted in all the states the individual has lived in the previous twenty years.

   c. Individuals must have regular involvement in the church for at least six months before being allowed to be a teacher or leader of children or youth.

5. Deal appropriately with offenders and allegations of abuse.

    a.   When a child discloses abuse or child abuse is suspected, Child Protective Services (United States: 1-800-4ACHILD or _____ [*the phone number for your state or province*]) or the police (911) will be notified at once. If there is uncertainty as to whether a situation requires reporting, it will be referred to the pastor, a church child protection team member, or other church leader knowledgeable in the area of child abuse. When notification of abuse is made, the pastor and/or a member of the child protection team will be informed at once. The alleged offender will be removed immediately from all responsibilities involving contact with children until the conclusion of the investigation. All parents whose children may have come into contact with the alleged offender will be notified within forty-eight hours that allegations have been made and reported to the authorities.

    b.   When child abuse allegations have been made, pastoral care will be offered to all involved, by the pastor and/or appropriate referrals will be made by a child protection team member.

    c.   Any individual who is known to have been convicted of a child sexual offense must not be allowed any unsupervised contact with children and may not be involved in children's or youth ministry (formal or informal).

    d.   All parents of children and youth must be notified if there is a registered sex offender attending church at the time this information becomes known. New families to the church must be notified of this information within two months of beginning to attend church.

Child abuse prevention within our other communities

1. As a church, we will participate in at least one outreach project each year that provides concrete goods to families in _____ (*name of city*).

2. As a church, we will participate in at least one outreach project each year that provides concrete goods to families outside the _____ (*name of city*) area.

This policy will be implemented and facilitated by a child protection team of at least two individuals, appointed by the congregation.

Appendix 5

Teaching *Let the Children Come*

Use this material to teach adults in a group setting, such as a Sunday school class or a small group. Because of its sensitive nature a good bit of thought needs to be given to: who teaches the class, how the class is advertised, where the class is held, and how the class is taught.

Be very thoughtful in selecting a teacher or facilitator for this class. I recommend that the teacher be a mental health professional or at least someone with knowledge of child abuse and neglect, and good skills in empathy and conflict management. The teacher needs to be prepared for the emotional reactions that are inevitable when discussing child abuse and neglect.

Second, in announcing that a class will be taught on child abuse and neglect, be proactive in reassuring everyone that no incident of child abuse or neglect is suspected to have prompted this class, if indeed that is the case. Present the importance of learning about child abuse and neglect before anything ever happens to a child.

Each class participant (or household) should have a copy of *Let the Children Come* so they may read the material prior to it being discussed. Besides enhancing the learning potential, knowing ahead of time what will be discussed helps set people at ease. This is especially important for individuals who have had personal experiences with child abuse and neglect.

Choose a classroom or setting where conversation will not be easily overheard by others, particularly children. Talk with class members to determine how to handle confidentiality. While the material itself is not confidential, any stories shared by class members may be. Children should not be present for this class; use careful judgment in allowing adolescents to be present.

Appendix 6

Candle Time and Sample Prayers

Candles represent light, life, and healing. Lighting a candle can help class members focus and create an atmosphere of worship and calm. Use a ring of eight candles in each session: three yellow and five green. The three yellow candles represent the child victim, the adult survivor, and the offender. The yellow candle representing the child should be smaller and placed in the ring with green candles on both sides. The second yellow candle represents the adult survivor of abuse and should also be placed with green candles on both sides. The third yellow candle represents the abuse offender; include it in the ring, but place it across the ring from the candles representing the child victim and adult survivor. The green candles represent everyone else, perhaps not touched personally by abuse but willing to be in community with those who have. Interweave green ivy through all the candles, representing God's love that enfolds us all.

Light the candles each class period. As a way of drawing different people into participation, a class participant can be asked ahead of time to light the candles. Minimize distractions as the candles are lit. Always light the smallest child candle first, then the candle representing the adult survivor, then the candle representing the offender; finally, light each green candle. Each time, remind class participants that the ivy interwoven throughout the candles represents the love of God enfolding us all.

Whether we are aware of it or not, there will likely be class participants who have experienced abuse or neglect as a child. We must be sensitive to the presence of these individuals, knowing that they may react emotionally to the material in a way that may seem like an overreaction or inappropriate. The candles can bring a sense of calm and healing and focus to these individuals. Since there will not always be time for participants to share their personal experiences of abuse and neglect, they can know that a candle is lit for them even if their story is not told this time.

Sample Prayer 1

As we light the first candle, we remember children everywhere who are being hurt by abuse and neglect.
Just as this candle is the smallest,
    so children are small,
        and vulnerable,
            and need our protection.

We light the second candle for all those young and old, who have been hurt by abuse and neglect in the past.
They may still be hurting,
    confused,
        angry.
They may be healing,
    ready to reach out
        ready to help others.

We light the third candle for those who have hurt others through abuse and neglect.
This candle is a safe distance from our child-candle.

This person may be struggling,
confused,
angry.
This person may be seeking love, wholeness, forgiveness
but doesn't know where to turn.

We light the green candles to represent the rest of us.
We may not have been hurt by someone we loved . . .
We may not have hurt a child with our actions
or our inactions . . .
Nevertheless, we are in the circle with those who have.
Together, we are community.

Finally, the ivy that surrounds us represents God's love.
God's love is here for all of us.
It encircles us, enfolds us, protects us.
Thanks be to God.

Sample Prayer 2

Lord, our God,

Today we think of children who have been hurt, bruised, even killed, by those closest to them. Our hearts go out to them. We acknowledge that children around us—those we see each week—may be hurting today. We confess that sometimes we have closed our eyes to their pain; . . . sometimes we haven't taken the time to see their pain; . . . or perhaps we just didn't recognize it. Please forgive us.

We also acknowledge today that some of us have been hurt by abuse and neglect in the past—maybe earlier this year, maybe a couple years ago, maybe decades ago. While the abuse is past, the pain is still present. We are reminded of it when we least expect it. Lord, heal us. Help us to trust again, to love again, to become whole again.

There are those among us who have hurt others—who have hurt children. Perhaps it was intentional, perhaps unin-

tentional. *Perhaps we didn't know what else to do. Lord, our God, help us to love, to forgive, to bring wholeness, to protect the vulnerable.*

As we gather in community, we are mindful of all those around us. We see them often, but we confess that we don't actually know them. Give us wisdom, courage, and strength to reach out, to protect the children.

We thank you, Lord, for your love. Love that never stops, that never hurts, that reaches out to us. Amen.

Sample Prayer 3

God of hope and healing,
today we think about Tamar.

We are furious with Amnon for his lust, and for his actions.
He didn't love Tamar. Not in the beginning, not in the end.
Instead he thought only of his own needs, his desire for power
*   and control.*
We are furious with Jonadab for his wicked plan,
for his complete disregard for Tamar.
What kind of a man would encourage his friend to do such
*   an evil deed?*

We mourn for Tamar, who was being obedient to her father,
*   and who attempted to reason with her attacker . . . twice.*
We wish we could have been there to protect Tamar.
We wish we could have been there to support her afterward.
*   To invite her to tell her story.*
*   To walk alongside her as she grappled with her pain.*
*   To demand justice for her.*

We wonder about Absalom too.
We appreciate his anger toward his half brother.
But we wish he had confronted his half brother . . .
*   without killing him.*

We wish he had offered a salve to Tamar's wounds
    and not asked her to pretend nothing happened.

God of hope and healing,
    are there Tamars around us?
Are there ways that we can protect the young girls and boys
    we come into contact with this week?
        In our families, our church, our neighborhood, our schools,
are there ways that we can offer healing to victims of sexual
    abuse?

We know, O God,
        that you detest acquitting the guilty and condemning
            the innocent.[1]
Are there ways we can hold sexual offenders accountable for
    their actions?
        Ways we can keep them from preying on more victims?
Are there ways we can prevent potential offenders from fostering
    such evil thoughts and plans, long before they act on them?

Help us, dear God, to
        "Speak up for those who cannot speak for themselves,
            for the rights of all who are destitute."[2]
        To "speak up and judge fairly;"
        To "defend the rights of the poor and needy."[3]
And help us remember Jesus' words,
"Whatever you did for one of the least of these brothers or
    sisters of mine,
        you did for me."[4]

In Jesus' name. Amen.

Sample Prayer 4

We welcome back the ring of candles.
Today, we learn more about child abuse and neglect.

We enter this time and place with many conflicted feelings.
We are deeply saddened that so many children have been hurt
 and are hurting right now.
We are angry.
   Why wasn't someone there to protect them? To care for
    them? To love them?
We are worried about the children in our lives.
   Are they safe?
   Are we doing enough to protect them?

At the same time, we feel thankful.
   Thankful that we are together,
      that we don't have to face the demon of abuse and
       neglect alone.
Thankful we are beginning to feel empowered.
   We know that we can do something to protect the vulnerable.
   We know that we are not alone in our struggle.

O God,
the sin of child neglect is hurting children in my community
today.
   Children are not getting their most basic needs met.
      I may not yet know these children, but they are around me.
      I don't know how to find them, to help them.
         O God, please help me.

The sin of physical abuse is also hurting children in my com-
munity today,
   perhaps in my own family,
      perhaps in my own heart.

Teach me to discipline appropriately,
*   to teach and not to hurt,*
*   to model the behavior I expect.*

O God,
Help me to walk in your ways.
Help me to parent well and to care for all the children I see,
*   even as you parent and care for me.*

Thank you. Amen.

See www.DovesNest.net/worship for more prayers and poems.

Appendix 7

Books for Children on Child Abuse and Neglect

(Preview any book before reading or giving to a child to ensure appropriate content.)

Burnett, Frances Hodgson. *The Secret Garden.* New York: Signet Classics, 2003. (Ages 9–12)

Federico, Julie K. *Some Parts Are Not for Sharing.* Mustang, OK: Tate Publishing, 2009. (Baby–preschool)

Freeman, Lory. *It's My Body: A Book to Teach Young Children How to Resist Uncomfortable Touch.* Seattle, WA: Parenting Press, 1984. (Ages 4–8)

Girard, Linda. *My Body is Private.* Park Ridge, IL: Albert Whitman & Company, 1984. (Ages 4–8)

Hansen, Diane. *Those are MY Private Parts.* Atlanta: Empowerment Productions, 2004. (Ages 4–8)

Holmes, Margaret M. *A Terrible Thing Happened: A Story for Children Who Have Witnessed Violence or Trauma.* Washington, DC: Magination Press/American Psychological Association, 2000. (Ages 4–8)

Johnson, Karen. *The Trouble with Secrets.* Seattle, WA: Parenting Press, 1986. (Ages 4–8)

King, Kimberly. *I Said No! A Kid-to-Kid Guide to Keeping Your Private Parts Private*. Weaverville, CA: Boulden Publishing, 2008. (Ages 9–12)

Kleven, Sandy. *The Right Touch: A Read-Aloud Story to Help Prevent Child Sexual Abuse*. Kirkland, WA: Illumination Arts Publishing Company, 1998. (Ages 4–8)

Loftis, Chris. *The Words Hurt: Helping Children Cope with Verbal Abuse*. Far Hills, NJ: New Horizon Press, 1997. (Ages 4–8)

Ottenweller, Jessie. *Please Tell! A Child's Story About Sexual Abuse*. Center City, MN: Hazelden Publishing, 1991. (Ages 4–8)

Spelman, Cornelia Maude. *Your Body Belongs to You*. Morton Grove, IL: Albert Whitman & Company, 2000. (Ages 4–8)

Appendix 8

Frequently Asked Questions on Background Checks

1. Why do I need to do a background check?

Background checks can identify individuals who have been convicted of crimes and/or have been identified as a child abuse offender. Until convicted, however, sex offenders do not show up on registries. In addition, background checks may not extend outside your state and most certainly do not extend outside your country. Even if all the background checks you run come back clean, you will never know how many child abuse offenders were deterred from victimizing children in your church because they knew they would be caught with the background check.

2. On whom do I need to run a background check?

Run background checks on all staff and volunteers of the church, especially those who have direct responsibility or interactions with children and youth. This includes pastors, youth leaders, and Sunday school teachers, as well as custodians, bus drivers, and nursery workers.

3. Do I need to let the individual know before I run a background check?

Yes. In order to process the request for a background check, you will need the individual's date of birth, place of birth, driver's license number, and/or Social Security number (U.S.).

4. How do I run a background check and how much will it cost?

At a minimum, you'll want to do a child abuse and neglect check. In the United States contact your state or county Health and Human Services (or Department of Family Services), and say you want to do a central registry check. (www.childwelfare.gov/systemwide/ laws_policies/statutes/centregall.pdf).

You can also do a criminal background check by going to the Church Mutual Insurance website (www.churchmutual.com) and gaining access to LexisNexis' ChoicePoint (www.choicepoint. com). The cost is less than $10.

In Canada contact your local police and ask for the procedures on running a background check.

If the staff member or volunteer will provide transportation for children or youth, you can also request a check through the Department of Motor Vehicles (DMV) (www.onlinedmv.com).

5. How can I check for sexual offenders in my community?

A. In the United States:
    1. United States Department of Justice, National Sex Offender Website, www.nsopw.gov
    2. www.sexoffender.com
    3. www.criminalsearches.com
    4. www.nationalalertregistry.com
    5. www.familywatchdog.us
B. In Canada: Contact local authorities.

Appendix 9

Church Checklist

Are you and your faith community prepared to end child abuse and neglect?

Are you:
___Aware that child abuse and neglect happens in our communities
___Knowledgeable of all types of child abuse and neglect, signs and symptoms, effects
___Familiar with community services:
  • Ready to make referrals to community services: know the name, address, phone numbers, directions, hours of operation, types of services offered, eligibility criteria
  • Know people who work in these agencies
  • Invite guest speakers from community agencies
  • Visit community agencies yourself

Do you:
___Know how to report child abuse and neglect
  (Phone _____)
___Know about the risk and protective factors for at risk children and families
___Volunteer or provide concrete resources through your church or a community agency
___Offer social support, within church, within your community

In addition, within your church do you:

____Have a child protection policy that is:
- Written, approved
- Made public
- Implemented; persons responsible: _____
- Signed by teachers and leaders once a year

____Complete education and training on child abuse prevention and safety
- For teachers, leaders, and parents once a year
- For children and youth

____Have a plan for what to do when a known sex offender attends your church

____Conduct background checks on all teachers and leaders

____Have a child abuse and neglect response plan

____Have a supervision plan, two-adult rule

____Have safe facilities:
- Safe environment inside and outside
- Windows in classroom doors and other internal doors
- First-aid kit

Notes

Foreword

1. Edward Zigler, "Controlling Child Abuse in America: An Effort Doomed to Failure," in *Proceedings of the First National Conference on Child Abuse and Neglect*, January 4-7, 1976 (Washington DC: U.S. Department of Health, Education and Welfare) 35.

2. A. J. Sedlak and others, *Fourth National Incidence Study of Child Abuse and Neglect (NIS–4): Report to Congress, Executive Summary* (Washington, DC: U.S. Department of Health and Human Services, Administration for Children and Families, 2010).

3. U.S. Department of Health and Human Services, Administration on Children, Youth and Families, *Child Maltreatment 2007* (Washington, DC: U.S. Government Printing Office, 2009).

4. Ibid.

5. Robert Wuthnow, *Acts of Compassion: Caring For Others and Helping Ourselves* (Princeton, NJ: Princeton University Press, 1991) 304.

Chapter 1: Dispelling Myths of Child Abuse and Neglect

1. U.S. Department of Health and Human Services, Administration on Children, Youth and Families, *Child Maltreatment 2008* (Washington, DC: U.S. Government Printing Office, 2010).

2. Nico Trocmé and others, *Canadian Incidence Study of Reported Child Abuse and Neglect-2003 (CIS-2003)* (Ottawa, ON: Minister of Public Works and Government Services Canada, 2005).

3. *Child Maltreatment 2008*. Percents add up to more than one hundred because some children were victims of more than one type of abuse or neglect.

4. Trocmé and others, *CIS-2003*.

5. *Child Maltreatment 2008.*

6. Statistics Canada, Canadian Centre for Justice Statistics, *Family Violence in Canada: A Statistical Profile* (Ottawa, ON: Statistics Canada, 2009), www.statcan.gc.ca/bsolc/olc-cel/olc-cel?catno=85-224-X&lang=eng.

7. "Missing Person and Unidentified Person Statistics for 2007," National Child Information Center, www.fbi.gov/hq/cjisd/missingpersons.htm.

8. *Child Maltreatment 2008.*

Chapter 3: What Does the Bible Say About Child Abuse and Neglect?

1. Amber Alert, America's Missing: Broadcast Emergency Response, www.amberalert.gov.

Chapter 4: Child Abuse and Neglect 101

1. Jill Goldman and others, *A Coordinated Response to Child Abuse and Neglect: The Foundation for Practice* (Washington, DC: Child Welfare Information Gateway, Office on Child Abuse and Neglect, HHS, 2003), www.childwelfare.gov/pubs/usermanuals/foundation/index.cfm.

2. Jim Albert and Margot Herbert, "Child Welfare," in *The Canadian Encyclopedia*, 2010, www.thecanadianencyclopedia.com.

3. Ben Mathews and Maureen C. Kenny, "Mandatory Reporting Legislation in the United States, Canada, and Australia: A Cross-Jurisdictional Review of Key Features, Differences, and Issues," in *Child Maltreatment 2008.*

4. "History of Child Welfare," Ontario Association of Children's Aid Societies, 2010, www.oacas.org/childwelfare/history.htm.

5. Goldman and others, *A Coordinated Response*, chap. 2.

6. *Child Maltreatment 2008.*

7. Trocmé and others, *CIS-2003.*

8. Statistics Canada, Canadian Centre for Justice Statistics, *Family Violence in Canada.*

9. Trocmé and others, *CIS-2003.*

10. Dennette Derezotes, John Poertner, and Mark F. Testa, eds, *Racial Disproportionality in the U.S. Child Welfare System:*

What We Know (2003–2005) (Washington, DC: Child Welfare League of America, 2005).

11. *Child Maltreatment 2008.*

12. *Child Maltreatment 2008.*

13. Conrad L. Kanagy, *Road Signs for the Journey: A Profile of Mennonite Church USA* (Scottdale, PA: Herald Press, 2007).

14. Isaac A. Block, *Assault on God's Image: Domestic Abuse,* (Winnipeg, MB: Windflower Communications, 1991).

15. Rodger R. Rice and Ann W. Annis, *A Survey of Abuse in the Christian Reformed Church* (Grand Rapids, MI: Social Research Center, 1992).

16. Patricia Moccia and David Anthony, eds, *The State of the World's Children* (New York: UNICEF, 2008), 24, www.unicef.org/rightsite/sowc/pdfs/SOWC_Spec%20Ed_CRC_Main%20Report_EN_090409.pdf.

17. *World Perspectives on Child Abuse: An International Resource Book*, 8th ed. (Chicago: International Society for Prevention of Child Abuse and Neglect, 2008), www.ispcan.org/wp/index.htm.

18. *Child Poverty in Perspective: An Overview of Child Well-Being in Rich Countries*, Report Card 7 (Florence, Italy: UNICEF Innocenti Research Centre, 2007), www.unicef-irc.org/publications/pdf/rc7_eng.pdf.

19. United Nations High Commissioner for Human Rights, "Convention on the Rights of the Child" (General Assembly resolution 44/25, 1989), www2.ohchr.org/english/law/crc.htm.

20. UNICEF, *Convention on the Rights of the Child*, 2006, www.unicef.org/crc/index_30229.html.

21. Rosemary Chalk, Alison Gibbons, and Harriet J. Scarupa, *The Multiple Dimensions of Child Abuse and Neglect: New Insights into an Old Problem* (Washington, DC: Child Trends, 2002), www.childtrends.org/Files/ChildAbuseRB.pdf.

22. *Long-term Consequences of Child Abuse and Neglect* (Washington, DC: Child Welfare Information Gateway, Office on Child Abuse and Neglect, HHS, 2008), www.childwelfare.gov.

Chapter 5: A Look at Neglect and Emotional Abuse

1. Trocmé and others, *CIS-2003.*

2. *Child Maltreatment 2008.*

3. Rebecca Toni, "Child Abuse and Neglect," in *National Data Analysis System: Issue Brief*, Child Welfare League of America (January 2006).

Chapter 6: A Look at Physical Abuse

1. *What Is Child Abuse and Neglect?* (Washington, DC: Child Welfare Information Gateway, Office on Child Abuse and Neglect, HHS, 2008), www.childwelfare.gov.
2. Sue Hille, "The Rod of Guidance," in *SCAN Advocate* (1985), www.faithtrustinstitute.org.
3. "Punish," dictionary.com, http://dictionary.reference.com/browse/punish.
4. "Discipline," dictionary.com, http://dictionary.reference.com/browse/discipline.

Chapter 7: A Look at Sexual Abuse

1. *What Is Child Abuse and Neglect?*
2. Kathleen Coulborn Faller, *Child Sexual Abuse: An Interdisciplinary Manual for Diagnosis, Case Management, and Treatment* (New York: Columbia University Press, 1988), 11.
3. Statistics Canada, Canadian Centre for Justice Statistics, *Family Violence in Canada*.
4. A. J. Sedlak and others, *Fourth National Incidence Study of Child Abuse and Neglect (NIS–4): Report to Congress, Executive Summary* (Washington, DC: U.S. Department of Health and Human Services, Administration for Children and Families, 2010).
5. Statistics Canada, Canadian Centre for Justice Statistics, *Family Violence in Canada*.

Chapter 8: Risk and Protective Factors

1. *Long-term Consequences of Child Abuse and Neglect*.
2. Susan Whitelaw Downs and others, *Child Welfare and Family Services: Policies and Practice*, 7th ed. (Boston: Pearson Education, 2004).
3. Statistics Canada, Canadian Centre for Justice Statistics, *Family Violence in Canada*.
4. *Child Maltreatment 2008*.

5. Holly Johnson, *Measuring Violence Against Women: Statistical Trends 2006* (Ottawa: Statistics Canada), 13, www.statcan.gc.ca/pub/85-570-x/85-570-x2006001-eng.pdf.

6. Statistics Canada, Canadian Centre for Justice Statistics, *Family Violence in Canada.*

7. Trocmé and others, *CIS-2003.*

Chapter 9: Offenders

1. *Child Maltreatment 2008.*

2. Cindy L. Miller-Perrin and Robin D. Perrin, *Child Maltreatment: An Introduction.* (Thousand Oaks, CA: Sage, 1999).

3. Ibid.

4. Statistics Canada, Canadian Centre for Justice Statistics, *Family Violence in Canada.*

5. Sedlak and others, *Fourth National Incidence Study of Child Abuse and Neglect (NIS–4).*

Chapter 10: Ending Child Abuse and Neglect in our Communities

1. Project Harmony, Omaha, Nebraska, www.projectharmony.com.

Chapter 11: Ending Child Abuse and Neglect in our Churches

1. Gregory Love and Kimberlee Norris, "Sexual Abuse Issues in the Church; Raising the Bar. Today's Children's Ministry," *Christianity Today* (April 4, 2008), 1, www.christianitytoday.com/childrensministry/operations/sexualabuseinthechurch.html?start=1.

2. Joy Thornburg Melton, *Safe Sanctuaries for Children and Youth: Reducing the Risk of Abuse in the Church* (Nashville: Discipleship Resources, 2004).

3. Joy Thornburg Melton, *Safe Sanctuaries for Ministers: Reducing the Risk of Abuse in the Church* (Nashville: Discipleship Resources, 2009).

4. United Methodist Church, *Conference Policy: Safe Sanctuaries*, www.safesanctuaries.org/conference_policy/index.html.

5. Christian Reformed Church, *Safe Church Ministry* (2010), http://www.crcna.org/pages/safechurch_index.cfm.

6. Mennonite Church Canada, *Volunteer Screening for a Safe Church* (2007), 3, www.mennonitechurch.ca/resourcecentre/FileDownload/8174/Volunteer_Screening_for_a_Safe_Church_2007.pdf.

7. Mennonite Church Canada, *Volunteer Screening Policy and Procedures Manual* (2010), 5, www.mennonitechurch.ca/resourcecentre/ResourceView/5/10018.

8. Mennonite Church USA Historical Committee (2003), www.mcusa-archives.org/library/resolutions/nooneshallmakethemafraid.html.

9. "Western District is Well on Its Way to Becoming a Safe Sanctuaries Conference," Western District Conference of Mennonite Church USA, http://site.mawebcenters.com/westerndistrictconference/WDC_is_becoming_a_SS_conference.pdf.

10. One Childhood Consulting, http://onechildhoodconsulting.com/default.aspx.

11. The Dove's Nest Collaborative: Mennonites Keeping Children Safe, www.DovesNest.net.

12. Child Abuse, Mennonite Central Committee, http://abuse.mcc.org/abuse/en/child.

13. Beth Swagman, *Results and Summary of the Child Safety Survey* (Christian Reformed Church in North America, 2010), http://network.crcna.org/content/safe-church/results-and-summary-child-safety-survey.

Chapter 12: Child Abuse Prevention Policies in our Churches

1. *Circle of Grace*, Archdiocese of Omaha, www.archomaha.org/pastoral/se/circle.html.

Appendix 4: Sample Child Protection and Abuse Response Policy

1. Nebraska Department of Health and Human Services, "What is Abuse and Neglect?" (Lincoln, NB, 2007), www.hhs.state.ne.us/cha/abuse.htm.

Appendix 6: Candle Time and Sample Prayers

1. Proverbs 17:15.
2. Proverbs 31:8.
3. Proverbs 31:9 (NIV).
4. Matthew 25:40 (TNIV).

For Further Reading

Updated website links can be found at www.DovesNest.net/ LetTheChildrenCome.

Abuse: Response and Prevention. A Guide for Church Leaders. Mennonite Central Committee (MCC), 2008. See www. mennonitechurch.ca/resourcecentre/ResourceView/2/10780.
Bless Our Children: Preventing Sexual Abuse. Faith Trust Institute, 1993. DVD. www.faithtrustinstitute.org/ store/01tA0000000M7rkIAC.
Child Maltreatment 2008. Child Welfare Information Gateway. United States Department of Health and Human Services, Administration on Children, Youth and Families, Children's Bureau, 2010. www.childwelfare.gov.
Child Poverty in Perspective: An Overview of Child Well-Being in Rich Countries, *UNICEF, Innocenti Research Centre, Report Card 7, 2007.* www.unicef-irc.org/publications/ pdf/rc7_eng.pdf.
Circle of Grace, Archdiocese of Omaha. http://protestant. cograce.org.
Convention on the Rights of the Child, *Office of the United Nations High Commissioner for Human Rights, 1989.* General Assembly resolution 44/25. www2.ohchr.org/ english/law/crc.htm.
Cunningham, Alison, and Linda Baker. *Little Eyes, Little Ears: How Violence Against a Mother Shapes Children as They Grow.* The Centre for Children and Families in the Justice System, National Clearinghouse on Family Violence, Public

Health Agency of Canada, 2007. www.lfcc.on.ca/little_eyes_little_ears.pdf

"Dealing with Child Abuse." "Close to Home." Scottdale, PA: Faith & Life Resources, n.d. See http://store.mpn.net/productdetails.cfm?PC=666.

Hear Their Cries: Religious Responses to Child Abuse. Faith Trust Institute, n.d. [DVD] See www.faithtrustinstitute.org/store/01tA0000000M7rjIAC.

Heggen, Carolyn H. Sexual Abuse in Christian Homes and Churches. Scottdale, PA: Herald Press, 1993.

Hille, Sue. "The rod of guidance." SCAN Advocate, 1985. www.faithtrustinstitute.org.

Melton, Joy Thornburg. Safe Sanctuaries for Children and Youth: Reducing the Risk of Abuse in the Church. Nashville: Discipleship Resources, 2004. www.safesanctuaries.org.

Melton, Joy Thornburg. Safe Sanctuaries for Ministers: Reducing the Risk of Abuse in the Church. Nashville: Discipleship Resources, 2009. www.safesanctuaries.org.

Miller, Melissa A. Family Violence: The Compassionate Church Responds. Scottdale, PA: Herald Press, 1994.

Moccia, Patricia and David Anthony, eds. The State of the World's Children, UNICEF, 2009, www.unicef.org/rightsite/sowc/pdfs/SOWC_Spec%20Ed_CRC_Main%20Report_EN_090409.pdf.

O'Neill, Erin M. O., Stephanie Huckins, Jodi Gabel, and Jeanette Harder. "Prevention of Child Abuse and Neglect Through Church and Social Service Collaboration," Social Work & Christianity, forthcoming.

Reid, Kathy Goering. Preventing Child Sexual Abuse: A Curriculum for Children Ages Five Through Eight. Nashville, TN: Pilgrim Press, 1994.

Reid, Kathy Goering. Preventing Child Sexual Abuse: A Curriculum for Children Ages Nine Through Twelve. Cleveland, OH: Pilgrim Press, 1990.

Swagman, Beth. Preventing Child Abuse. Grand Rapids, MI: CRC Publications, 1997. www.crcna.org/safechurch.

Trocmé, Nico, Barbara Fallon, Bruce MacLaurin, Joanne Daciuk, Caroline Felstiner, Tara Black, Lil Tonmyr, Cindy Blackstock, Ken Barter, Daniel Turcotte, and Richard Cloutier. *Canadian Incidence Study of Reported Child Abuse and Neglect-2003 (CIS-2003)*. Minister of Public Works and Government Services Canada, 2005. http://origin.phac-aspc.gc.ca/ncfv-cnivf.

World Perspectives on Child Abuse; An International Resource Book, 8th ed. International Society for Prevention of Child Abuse and Neglect, 2008. www.ispcan.org/wp/index.htm.

Helpful Organizations

Updated website links can be found at www.DovesNest.net/ LetTheChildrenCome.

Anabaptist Disabilities Network: www.adnetonline.org
Canadian Child Welfare Research Portal: www.cecw-cepb.ca
Child Welfare Information Gateway: www.childwelfare.gov
Child Welfare League of America: www.cwla.org
Circles of Support and Accountability: in the United States, http://peace.fresno.edu/cosa; in Canada, http://alberta.mcc.org/programs/rjm/cosa
Court Appointed Special Advocates (CASA): www.nationalcasa.org
Darkness to Light: www.darknesstolight.org
The Dove's Nest Collaborative: www.DovesNest.net
Faith Trust Institute: www.faithtrustinstitute.org
FRIENDS, National Resource Center for Child Abuse Prevention: www.friendsnrc.org
Healthy Families America: www.healthyfamiliesamerica.org
Mennonite Central Committee: http://abuse.mcc.org/abuse/en/child
National Children's Alliance (Children's Advocacy Centers): www.nationalchildrensalliance.org
National Clearinghouse on Family Violence, Public Health Agency of Canada: www.phac-aspc.gc.ca/ncfv-cnivf

National Exchange Club Foundation: www.preventchildabuse.com
One Childhood Consulting: http://onechildhoodconsulting.com
Parents Anonymous: www.parentsanonymous.org
Prevent Child Abuse America: www.preventchildabuse.org
Religion and Violence eLearning (RAVE): www.theraveproject.org
Safe Sanctuaries: www.safesanctuaries.org
Statistics Canada: www.statcan.gc.ca
Tamar's Voice: www.tamarsvoice.org
VIRTUS Online: www.virtus.org/virtus

The Author

Jeanette Harder has a bachelor's degree in Bible and a master's degree and PhD in social work. She has conducted research in child abuse and neglect prevention for ten years.

Jeanette grew to know and love children and families touched by child abuse through her many years as a home visitor and foster parent. She is on faculty at the Grace Abbott School of Social Work at the University of Nebraska at Omaha.

Jeanette is an active member of First Mennonite Church in Lincoln, Nebraska. Jeanette is married to Stan; together they have a son who came to them by open adoption.